All-Color Guide

Paper
Money

of the World   Richard G. Doty

A Ridge Press Book

Bantam Books
Toronto · New York · London

Photo Credits

All photographs by Joseph D. Garcia

All bills obtained courtesy the collection of the American Numismatic Society,
New York, except the following:
Eric P. Newman Numismatic Education Society,
9, 118; Ron MacIntyre, The Clearing House (Stroudsburg, Pa.),
49, 64, 140, 142, 146, 147; Miguel Muñoz, 137;
Osram Vacublitz, 140.

PAPER MONEY OF THE WORLD
A Bantam Book published by arrangement with The Ridge Press.
Designed and produced by The Ridge Press. All rights reserved.
Copyright 1977 in all countries of the International Copyright Union by
The Ridge Press. This book may not be reproduced in whole
or in part by mimeograph or by any other means, without permission.
For information address: The Ridge Press,
25 W. 43 Street, New York, N.Y. 10036.
Library of Congress Catalog Card Number: 77-83907
ISBN 0-553-11568-5
Published simultaneously in the United States and Canada

Bantam Books are published by Bantam Books, Inc.
Its trademark, consisting of the words "Bantam Books" and the portrayal
of a bantam, is registered in the United States Patent Office
and in other countries. Marca Registrada.
Bantam Books, Inc., 666 Fifth Avenue, New York, N.Y. 10019
Printed in Italy by Mondadori Editore, Verona

Contents

▼ *Manchuria, 100 yuan, 1939.*

Introduction

Paper-money collecting is the fastest-growing area in the field of numismatics. Ten years ago, there were virtually no clubs or learned organizations devoted to paper money, but today there are dozens. In those same ten years, we have seen the values of many bills double, and double again. Both of these facts point to an upsurge of collector interest in paper money.

What attraction does paper hold for a collector? Why are there so many more paper-money enthusiasts now than there were only a few years ago? First, the world has largely become an economy based on paper. The United States is a good example. At one time there were coinage denominations up to twenty dollars, but times changed and so did the American economy. The higher-value coins were gradually replaced by paper money representing the same amounts. Now, for amounts more than one dollar, paper is used. And while we still have a dollar coin, it is regarded as something of an oddity by the general public and it doesn't circulate. We've become used to paper, in part because of its greater convenience, in part because our government tells us that it has value and we believe our government. (This faith in the value of paper money is essential, as we shall see.) What has happened in the United States has also taken place throughout the rest of the world. And it is only natural that as the use of paper money has become universal, the ranks of those collecting it have grown.

4 But there are other, special reasons for the growth in popu-

Top: Central Bank of China, yuan, 1936;
bottom: Tahiti, 5,000 francs, 1969 (specimen). ▶

larity of the field. Overall, paper-money collecting is a most satisfying hobby. Despite the rise in prices, most paper is still well within reach of the average collector. Paper money is available from places that never issued coins. And more than coins, paper money can tell a story about the ever-changing tastes and fortunes of the people who made it.

However, there is one basic reason for the popularity of paper-money collecting: it's easier and cheaper to print paper than it is to strike coins—in terms of time, equipment, labor, and cost. Thus, for the average collector, there is a good deal more paper money available than there are coins. And much of it is old—it's perfectly possible to obtain a bill printed over a

▲ Greece, 100 billion drachmae, 1944.

5

century ago, in good condition, for only a few dollars. An amazing amount of old paper money has survived, and the modern collector can reap the benefits.

Moreover, since paper money is easier to produce than coins, a great number of short-lived groups and governments have printed it. Though their coins may be rare or nonexistent, their paper may be common. Prime examples of this are the factions that were active during the Mexican Revolution (1910–20) and the Russian Civil War (1917–24). The collector can choose from a wide variety of paper, much of it of great interest, almost all of it low priced. In effect, his or her collecting horizons widen when specializing in paper money.

Finally, paper money can tell us a great deal about the past, perhaps more than coins can. Because it is easy to produce, it is not tied to the static designs that are the lot of coinage. It can reflect artistic tastes, patriotic ideals, ways of life. A note from the State Bank of New Brunswick is a capsule commentary on America around 1860. The style is ornate and florid, reflecting artistic tastes of the period. The idealized figure in the center vignette shows us what their beauty standards may have been. The shield on the reverse represents the deep-seated patriotism that was typical of America during this age. And the engravings on the left and right sides of the face give us an idea of how people made their livings in those long-gone days. So it is with all paper money, past and present: it can give us glimpses of what people are like, how they live, and what they would like to become.

▲ Cuba, 5 pesos, 1869.

FIFTY CENTS

HEPPNER SHEEPSKIN SCRIP

50   № G 0326   50c

Issued by the Business Men of Heppner, Oregon

FIFTY CENTS

Heppner Gazette Times

Paper can tell us other things, too. It can speak with eloquence of the heart-breaking economic inflation that ruins an entire economy: a Greek note for one hundred *billion* drachmas does so. It can speak of great heroes of the past, as does the beautiful, multicolored five-thousand-franc note of Tahiti; or of the national past itself, as does the charming engraving of a company of travelers on a Chinese yuan (dollar) of 1936. It can record the travail of the birth of new nations, as does an 1869 Cuban five-peso note, printed by insurgents. Their revolt against Spanish rule failed, but their notes remain. Paper can bear mute testimony to national or local emergencies, as does a fifty-cent note from a small town in Oregon, printed there *on leather* in 1933, during the depths of the Great Depression, when coins were widely hoarded. When we consider that paper can do all this, plus be esthetically pleasing, printed in bright colors, we can readily see why it is growing in popularity.

This book is an introduction to paper money for the beginning collector, but it will also aid the more experienced hobbyist. It will cover as much of the field as possible, with an emphasis on low- to moderately priced material. Happily, this approach embraces most paper money. We'll discuss how to build a collection, how to store it, etc. First, however, we must examine the growth of the use of paper money itself, a worldwide development occupying more than one thousand years.   **7**

▲ *Heppner, Oregon, 50 cents, 1933.*

A History of Paper Money

The idea of using a piece of paper to represent a certain amount of money is a sophisticated one. The usage of paper today comes as no surprise; we are accustomed to it and tend to take it for granted. What *is* surprising is the fact that it is not a new concept. We can trace its roots back through thirteen centuries of history.

Unlike coinage, there is no dispute as to who invented paper money. It was the Chinese, and according to literary evidence, they did so sometime in the seventh century. Both the T'ang and the later Sung dynasties used it. The rulers of the latter house soon discovered one of the basic problems involved in a paper currency: if too much of it is printed, people tend not to accept it at face value, and if overproduction continues, there is likely to be public unrest. In fact, the overissue of paper money by the Sung dynasty was a major factor in its overthrow in 1278, and in that of its successor, the Yüan. It was during the Yüan that an inquisitive traveler named Marco Polo arrived in China, observed the use of paper, and duly reported the new form of money on his return to Italy. Europeans would not take advantage of this idea for several hundred years, however.

All early Chinese banknotes are rare. They become somewhat more common during the Ming dynasty (1368–1644). The note illustrated was made during that period, printed with a woodblock on paper made from mulberry bark (ordinary paper—and the printing press—would not come along for another few hundred years). The Japanese were also pioneers in paper money: their first notes, issued in the fourteenth century, are often called "bookmarks" by collectors, due to their shape. Japanese notes from the eighteenth and nineteenth centuries, the close of the feudal period, are occasionally found today, but earlier examples are fairly rare.

The oriental experiment with paper currency did not directly influence its development in Europe. A literate minority had read or heard about Marco Polo's discovery, but paper money would be a separate European development, not a direct descendant of the Chinese financial experiment. While several reasons can be advanced for the absence of European imitation of Chinese currency, one single fact stands out:

◄ Foreground: Japan, mon, c. 1725; background: China, 1,000 cash, c. 1400.
▼ Massachusetts, "20" shillings, 1690.

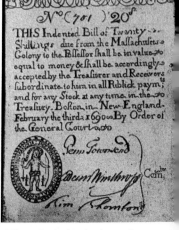

No (701) 20ˢ

THIS Indented Bill of Twenty Shillings due from the Massachusets Colony to the Possessor shall be in value equal to money & shall be accordingly accepted by the Treasurer and Receivers subordinate to him in all Publick paymᵗˢ; and for any Stock at any time in the Treasury. Boston in New England February the third 1690. By Order of the General Court

Penn Townsend
Adam Winthrop   Comⁱᵗᵉ
Tim Thornton

◄ Above: Bank of England, pound, 1810; below: bill of exchange, 1779.

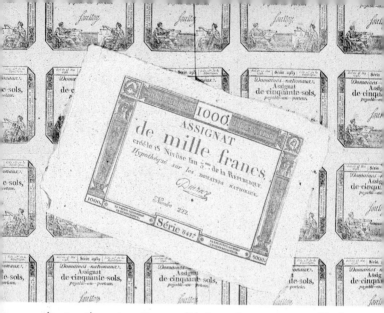

fourteenth-century Europe didn't need paper money. Trade existed by barter, or when necessary by the use of coins.

But as Europe began advancing from the Middle Ages, trade revived; and with it, European paper money was born. Its development went hand in hand with advances in banking and commerce, and paper currency came into use as bankers and businessmen began looking for easier ways to carry on a growing amount of trade.

The earliest form of European paper money was the promissory note, or bill of exchange. Its operation was simple: *A* promised to pay *B* a specified sum of money. *B* soon discovered that, provided *A* was a merchant of repute with a good credit rating, he could use *A*'s note for his own purchase. And so it went. This bill of exchange simplified business transactions a great deal, for it meant that large sums of money could be exchanged without having to be transported all over Europe, a fairly risky business in those days. It could all be done on paper. Governments, too, came to use the bill of exchange. The note illustrated, though it was used much later, is an example: it is an early product of the United States **10** government, and it was endorsed by Francis Hopkinson, one

▲ *France, assignats, 1793–95.*

◀ Above: United States, 50 dollars, 1778; below: British counterfeit of the same note.
▼ Left: France, siege note, 1793; right: Sweden, 8 skilling, 1825.

of the signers of the Declaration of Independence.

From the bill of exchange, the transition to real paper money was a short one. Sweden seems to have pioneered it in 1661, and the English soon followed in 1695. There was extreme conservatism in the style of the English paper money: the ten-pound note shown dates from 1810, but it could have been issued more than a century earlier. Other countries in Europe soon began experimenting with the new medium, and by 1750, paper currency had an assured place in their economies. It was also a somewhat dubious position, as we shall see.

Paper money soon popped up in an unlikely locale—the struggling, infant British colonies in America. Necessity, not convenience, drove them to adopt the new invention almost as soon as it was devised. Massachusetts and the other colonies lacked native gold or silver for coinage, and by the late seventeenth century, they were developing rapidly enough so that simple barter was no longer sufficient for their needs. Massachusetts, the economic leader of that time, decided to experiment with an issue of paper in 1690. The scheme worked fairly well, and other colonies soon imitated it.

If Americans were one of the first to use paper money, they

▲ Top to bottom: Uruguay, 20 pesos 1871; Brasil,
  2 mil reis, late 1880s; China, International Banking
  Association, 5 dollars, 1905 (specimen).
◀ Peru, 1,000 pesos, c. 1860 (trial printing).

▲ *Russia, 500 rubles, 1912.*

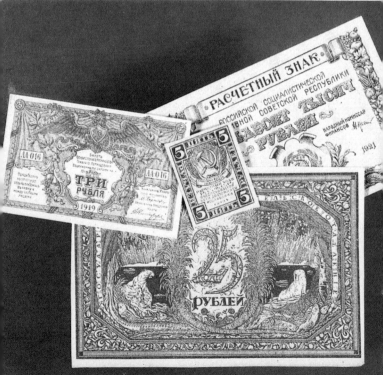

were also one of the first to encounter two problems inherent in the medium, problems that they were unable to solve—and, for that matter, problems that no one else has solved, either.

To begin, if paper money was easy for a government to manufacture, it soon became apparent that it wasn't especially difficult for anyone else to manufacture. The illustration of the 1690 Massachusetts note tells the tale. The note is genuine, but someone carefully raised its value from two to twenty shillings with a pen and ink. Out-and-out counterfeits shortly appeared, which occasioned increasingly elaborate attempts by colonial authorities to produce bills that could *not* be counterfeited. (One of the reasons why governments today print their bills in beautiful, elaborate designs is to ward off counterfeiting.)

If private individuals can counterfeit currency, so can governments. During the American Revolution, England extensively counterfeited American paper money in an attempt to decrease its value and hamper the American war effort. One of their productions is shown, along with the genuine United States note it sought to discredit. This was one of the earliest instances of economic warfare, and it would be duplicated in many future conflicts.

Counterfeiting was a definite problem with the new medium of exchange, as Americans found to their sorrow. Inflation was another. The secret of paper money is a prosaic one: if the average person believes that a bill is worth what his government says it's worth, if he believes that his government can—and will—redeem its paper if necessary, then paper will circulate at a stable value. But if governments print too much of it or are unable or unwilling to redeem what they've already issued, then public faith declines along with the value of the currency. Inflation was a constant problem in American colonial days, and it got totally out of hand during the American Revolution, so much so that the entire United States monetary system collapsed and had to be replaced. And this experience, too, would be duplicated in many other countries.

France experienced it late in the eighteenth century, during the age of the *assignats*. Assignats were paper currency issued by the French Revolutionary governments to pay for the national war effort. They were theoretically backed by the value **15**

◀ Clockwise from top: Soviets, 50,000 rubles, 1921;
Archangel, 25 rubles, 1918; South Russia, 3
rubles, 1919; center: Soviets, 5 rubles, 1921.

of lands taken from the Roman Catholic church. Unfortunately, the costs of waging war against virtually the rest of Europe rose steadily, and the French government, lacking gold or silver to pay its expenses, simply printed more and more assignats. By the middle of the 1790s, something like fifty billion livres' worth of the new money was in circulation, a value many times in excess of the entire wealth of France. With great difficulty the government recalled the worthless assignats and switched to coinage. But many people never returned them and today they are readily available to the modern collector for a few dollars each.

Paper money reflected the political uncertainties of the times. Never was this truer than during the struggles of the Napoleonic Wars (1792–1815), a direct outgrowth of the French Revolution. The assignats are one example of the close relationship between money and world events. Another example are siege notes, paper money issued by towns surrounded and besieged by enemy armies. The note illustrated is typical; it was printed by the defenders of Mainz, Germany, in May, 1793.

16

▲ *Top: 50 mark, 1914; lower left: 100,000 mark, 1923; lower right: 5 trillion mark, 1924.*

Early nineteenth-century paper money was still primitive by modern standards. Notes were often printed from movable type, as shown by a Swedish eight-schilling specie issue of 1825. And if they were printed from engraved plates, in the manner of modern paper money, they were simple. Ornamentation was limited, as was the use of vignettes—small engravings of persons or things that make up a prominent part of the design of modern notes. Most paper money was printed in one color—black.

By the middle of the century, all this was changing. Technological developments were partly responsible, for it became possible to do more ornate, detailed engraving. This was just as well, for the counterfeiters were getting better at their craft, too. Moreover, as the use of paper money spread throughout the world, it suddenly became profitable to get the finest craftsmen and machinery available and set up a firm solely devoted to the printing of money for governments, banks, and businesses. Most of the great banknote printing corporations of Europe and the United States have their roots in this period.

▲ *Typical German notgeld, 1921–23.*

Further sophistications followed. The early multicolored notes tended to use colors only in specific, highly limited parts of the overall design. This can be seen on a Peruvian trial-printing note, which dates from around 1860. More subtle use of color printing came along shortly, as on the Uruguayan and Brasilian pieces depicted. By the time of the latter note, about 1885, the general format that paper money would maintain until about 1960 had been achieved. Its usage was not confined to Europe or the Americas: the International Banking Corporation printed a five-dollar note for use in China, where the saga of paper money had started out in the first place.

Paper money has reflected the rising tensions of the twentieth century, and it may be one of the most representative objects of our century. In Russia, it has mirrored the epochal sweep of events that brought about the death of the Tsarist monarchy and the birth of a new era, that of the Soviet Union.

The notes illustrated speak eloquently of these matters. The first, a five-hundred-ruble note, dates from a few years before the Russian Revolution, and in its ornate, multicolored design we see something of the grandeur of Imperial Russia. These bills were printed in huge quantities to pay for Russian participation in World War I, and it was Russian involvement in that holocaust that brought on the 1917 Revolution.

In 1917, Civil War erupted in the former Russian Empire. Dozens of groups and armies contended for mastery, and in order to finance their efforts, many of them printed paper money. Several of their products are illustrated here. By the early 1920s, the Bolsheviks had gained an uneasy control over most of Russia, but by this time, the constant printing of excessive amounts of paper money had led to rampant inflation, as this Soviet note for fifty thousand rubles attests. Russia's currency would finally be reformed three years later, but not without great difficulty for the new regime.

But if inflation was a problem for Soviet Russia, it was a catastrophe in several other countries, most notably Germany and Hungary. Like Russia, Germany had printed paper money to fight World War I. Provided she were victorious, there would be little trouble in paying off her obligations. She lost **18** the war, and this, along with distrust of the new republican government, precipitated a fall in the value of the German mark that got progressively worse as time went on. The figures are graphic: at the outbreak of war in 1914, it took 4.2 marks to buy a dollar; by 1918, 8.4; by 1920, about 55; and by early 1924, 4.2 *trillion*. By that time, people had simply given up using money and had reverted to barter.

Top to bottom: 5 pengo, 1939; same denomination as a silver coin, 1938; 200 septillion pengo, 1946.

As national currency had become increasingly suspect, German cities, towns, and businesses had began to issue money of their own. This type of currency is called *notgeld*, and it, too, reflected the progressive economic chaos of the times. It is, however, a boon for the paper-money collector, for much of it is colorful and virtually all of it is inexpensive.

By 1924, the German economy was in a shambles. Borrowing from abroad, the government reformed the currency that year, and the German mark recovered a measure of its prewar reputation. But the topsy-turvy world of the inflation years, when it took a wheelbarrow-load of paper money to buy a loaf of bread, made an indelible impression on the German people. It bred a cynicism towards their government that helped pave the way for Adolf Hitler.

Twenty years later, a somewhat similar set of circumstances produced the worst inflation the world has ever seen, in Hungary. The basic Hungarian unit of exchange was called a pengo. In 1938, it took roughly five of them to buy a dollar. Hungary entered World War II, lost, and by 1945–46 was experiencing much the same sort of inflation as had Germany twenty years earlier, only much worse. By the end of May, 1946, a note for two hundred *septillion* pengo had appeared. (That's a two followed by twenty-six zeroes!) At that point, the Hungarian government scrapped the old monetary system, and with massive aid from the United States and the Soviet Union, erected a new one in its place. But much damage had been done: as in Germany, rampant inflation helped bring down the old government and replace it with a new one, a Communist dictatorship. Inflation is still with us today, and it probably will be as long as we use paper money. But it is unlikely to match the experiences of Germany and Hungary.

Today's paper money is perhaps the most attractive ever issued, employing clean, modern designs and a multicolor printing process. Unlike earlier days, much of it is now printed in the country of issue. The Brasilian fifty-cruzeiro bill of 1970 is an excellent example of a modern, locally produced note. It shows a recent trend in paper money around the world—from Switzerland to Afghanistan—the use of an abundance of national heroes and patriotic scenes.

*Top to bottom: Afghanistan, 20 afghanis, 1961; Brasil,
50 cruzeiros, 1970 (specimen); Switzerland, 100 francs, 1965.*

The British Isles

The paper money of England, Scotland, Ireland, and the rest of the British Isles have a number of striking similarities. All regions saw early issues of paper money, both on the public and private level. The paper money of each was marked by a great deal of conservatism—in the unchanging types and designs—until fairly recent times. Finally, when designs were modernized, they tended to be in the direction of simple elegance, the result being that the present paper money of the British Isles is among the most handsome now being produced.

As we have seen, England's paper currency commenced with the first issues of the Bank of England, one of the world's foremost banking institutions, in 1695. The Bank's early productions were generally simple in design, printed in black, and on paper with an elaborate watermark (a design pressed into the paper during its manufacture, an anticounterfeiting device). They employed a single vignette at the upper left, and the overall size tended to be quite large. The illustration shows the extremely conservative, static nature of this currency.

While the semipublic Bank of England was producing these notes, private banks were producing their own currencies. Many of these private banknotes closely resembled Bank of England issues—sometimes deliberately—as bankers wished to confuse the public in order to pass their notes, which might or might not be as valuable as those of the Bank of England.

Eventually, about seven hundred private banks were printing paper money, which caused a good deal of confusion and uncertainty on the part of the public. Further, the lack of effective centralized control over banking practices led to periodic crashes and massive bank failures, the worst of which took place in 1825–26, when hundreds of banks went under. Their issues are popular today with currency collectors, and since many of the notes could not be redeemed at the time and were saved, they are often available at moderate prices.

Due to economic problems and belated governmental restrictions, the number of note-issuing banks steadily declined throughout the nineteenth and early twentieth centuries. The last of them disappeared in England shortly after World War I.

Top to bottom: Windsor Bank, pound, 1815; Cornish Bank, 5 pounds, 1878; Wolverhampton Bank, pound, 1815. ▶

▲ Bank of England. Top: 10 pounds, 1833; bottom: 5 pounds, 1938.

That conflict brought about a change in the English paper-money system. Alarmed at the possibility of a banking crisis at the outbreak of war in 1914, the British government began issuing their own paper currency, called treasury notes, in ten-shilling and one-pound denominations. The pound note illustrated dates from 1919, and its design, far more elaborate than anything produced up to that time by the Bank of England, was continued with minor changes until mid-1933, when the treasury notes were called in.

By this time the Bank of England was updating its own designs. Higher denominations continued to employ the familiar black-on-white format, but pound and ten-shilling issues were now printed in a variety of colors. By the early 1960s, the entire series of designs used on Bank of England notes had been revamped, and an issue of truly outstanding designs, in denominations from ten shillings to twenty pounds, came into production. Many of them depicted scenes or heroes from England's past, and all of them bore the portrait of the current ruler. The subtle, pleasing multicolor designs have **24** made English paper money popular with collectors.

▲ *Top: treasury note, pound, 1919;*
bottom: Bank of England, pound, 1950's.

A curious feature of the paper currency of the British Isles is that, while England and Ireland have both issued paper money, so have Scotland, Northern Ireland, and several other component parts of the United Kingdom. The history of this paper money tends to parallel that of English productions in many respects: a fair degree of conservativism in design, a large number of private, or "wildcat," banks, and then more modern currency with attractive, locally inspired designs.

Scottish private banks began printing paper money shortly after their English counterparts. Designs tended to be simple at first, but by the middle of the nineteenth century increasingly elaborate designs were adopted. The official Bank of Scotland produced a number of banknotes of mediocre design, whose predominant colors, once the simple black on white of earlier years had been replaced, were generally various shades of yellow-brown. As time went on, two things happened: the number of Scottish banks printing paper money declined; and all banks, public and private, began upgrading their designs. Modern Scottish notes portray authors and heroes, local scenery, and other elements of a rising Scottish sense of national- **25**

▲ *Modern Bank of England notes. Top: pound,*
 1970 to present; bottom: 5 pounds, 1971.

ity. The same general process may be observed elsewhere, in such disparate places as the Channel Islands, the Isle of Man, and Northern Ireland.

The picture is somewhat different for the rest of Ireland. After a long and bloody civil war, the southern three-quarters of Ireland became independent in 1922, styling itself the Irish Free State. As part of the United Kingdom, Ireland had seen a large number of private, note-issuing banks, similar to those found elsewhere in the British Isles. As a free republic, however, it was decided that Ireland should have a distinct national currency. Thus, while the British monetary standard was retained for convenience, new, typically Irish designs were adopted for the new notes of the Currency Commission and the other agencies responsible for printing Ireland's paper money. Moreover, in an attempt to heighten the sense of nationhood of the Irish people, it was decided that each note should be printed in two languages, English and Gaelic—and all Irish paper money has been printed in these two languages ever since. The first Irish national currency was produced in 1928, and its release to the public coincided with the appearance of the Free State's first coinage. Irish paper money has remained virtually unchanged since its introduction almost fifty years ago.

Any discussion of the paper money of Ireland must include **26** an interesting series of notes issued by the Fenians, an Irish

▲ *Top: Royal Bank of Scotland, pound, 1975;*
below: Central Bank of Scotland, 10 pounds, c. 1860 (specimen).

nationalist group of the mid-1860s. The Fenians wanted to free Ireland from English rule. To finance their operations, they had paper money printed in New York City, a center of anti-English, pro-Irish sentiment at that time. Specifically, the paper money was intended to pay for a projected invasion of Canada, which hopefully would embroil the United States and Great Britain in a war. If that happened, Americans might help Ireland to achieve her independence. The scheme probably never had a chance, but it looked feasible in the beginning. After all, there was a large amount of anti-British sentiment on the part of many Americans, originating with the American Revolution and then greatly increased by British partiality towards the South during the Civil War.

So, the paper was issued, redeemable six months after "the independence of the Irish nation," and the Fenians got their invasion of Canada underway. Of course, after they were promptly stopped cold by Canadian and American forces, the movement sputtered out. Only these bills remain, a curious memento of an early attempt to free Ireland. Fenian paper money is quite popular with collectors. It is becoming increasingly difficult to find, but it's well worth the effort.

▲ Fenian currency, 1866.
◀ Top: Isle of Man, pound, 1939; bottom: Ireland 10 shillings, 1938.

France

France was one of the first European countries to experiment with paper money. She was also one of the first to experience rampant inflation, a danger inherent in the new medium of exchange.

The man responsible for the introduction of paper money in France, as well as for a number of unsound economic theories regarding its usage, was a Scotsman named John Law. Law founded the first modern French bank in 1716, and his creation, called the Banque Générale, issued the first French currency.

But Law was involved in other activities, too, and these brought about his downfall. He organized the French Mississippi Company of Louisiana in 1718, and this get-rich-quick scheme, a speculator's dream, came crashing down around his ears two years later. Thousands of people were ruined, and John Law had to flee the country. Unfortunately, his economic theories remained behind, and they would be resurrected seventy years later, producing the assignats.

The Scotsman had argued in favor of a land currency, equal to the value of French real estate, to pass at par with coined money. Unlike coinage, however, this land currency should not be subject to a fall in value. By the late 1780s, the royal French government was almost bankrupt, and Law's scheme was rediscovered, dusted off, and adopted as official policy. It gave France, and paper-money collectors, the assignats.

The first assignats appeared during the French Revolution, in 1789, and their value was backed by lands expropriated from the Church. Theoretically, they would circulate at parity with coinage, but they would be better than coinage, for they would pay five percent interest. What happened next was predictable. The French printed assignats to pay governmental expenses, and they were unable or unwilling to redeem their paper. Public acceptance of assignats declined.

By 1792, France was at war with virtually the rest of Europe. She still had not straightened out her internal finances, and she simply printed more assignats to pay for the conflict. By this time, the notes no longer bore interest, and the public accepted them only with great reluctance and only at a fraction

▲ *Assignats. Above: 80 livres, 1790; below: 25 livres, 1792.*

▲ *Banque de France, 50 francs, 1894.*

of their nominal value. France was locked into an inflationary spiral that Americans had seen a few years earlier, and that dozens of countries would see in the decades to come.

When France replaced Louis XVI with a republic, there were no immediate changes in fiscal policies. It did produce a curious series of assignats which, although they made reference to the new republic, also carried a vignette of Louis XVI, along with his title as king. That bit of inconsistency was settled in early 1793, when the luckless ex-monarch was beheaded.

France continued to issue assignats until 1797, when the government simply gave up printing them. It could be argued that the wild inflation of the First French Republic paved the way for a more authoritarian form of government, the First Empire of Napoleon.

The Napoleonic dictatorship (1799–1815) saw a moderate amount of paper money of the types illustrated, along with the establishment of private, note-emitting banks, such as the Banque de Rouen. Paper-money production was limited through the Napoleonic period and well beyond. The French did not forget how they had been injured by paper money, and they were not about to risk it happening a second time. Thus, **30** unlike the earlier assignats, later nineteenth-century paper

▲ Top: 250 francs, 1801; bottom: 500 francs, 1802.

money is fairly difficult to locate and quite expensive. France was firmly committed to a coin-based economy, and it would remain so through the rest of the nineteenth century and into the twentieth.

As in other countries, paper money began replacing coinage in the twentieth century. The agency responsible was the Banque de France. Organized in 1800, the Banque de France was given the authority to print paper money in high denominations, and it did so sparingly for the next fifty years. Its powers were increased by 1848 statutes, in which its currency was made legal tender for all public and private debts. As the century wore on, it assumed a monopoly on paper-money production, along with the authority to print lower-denomination notes. One of its early, typical issues is illustrated, a fifty-franc note of 1894. Most early Banque de France issues were printed in one or two colors, and they tended to be large sized.

The approach of World War I precipitated a crisis in the French economy. Uncertainty about the future led to widespread hoarding of money, including low-denomination coinage. This monetary shortage lasted from 1914 until the middle 1920s. Faced with this predicament, cities and towns **31**

▲ Banque de Rouen, 500 francs, 1807.

all over France printed small notes called *bons* or *billets,* the equivalent of the better-known German notgeld.

Bons were ordinarily printed in denominations of two francs or under, and they were simply municipal promises to pay on or after a certain date. They usually bore the signature of the mayor or some other person in authority. The earliest bons were primitive affairs, but towns soon began adding local **32** color to their notes, and the printing processes also became

Banque de France, 50 francs, 1938. ▶

more sophisticated. This was partially because many cities were having their bills printed by large, centralized printing plants in Paris and elsewhere.

The 1914 bon from Epernay is typical of the first issues; the other two, from Strasbourg and Nice, are representative of later productions. The Strasbourg note is particularly interesting as a bit of political propaganda. The central vignette shows a joyous France welcoming back her children, Alsace and Lorraine, lost to her in the Franco-Prussian War of 1870. And the note is dated 11 November 1918, the day World War I ended. The 1920 bon from Nice is outstanding because of its multicolored printing. It is probable that, by this time, *bons* were being printed for sale to collectors, in addition to their very real purpose as emergency money. The same thing was happening in Germany, as we shall see. French notgeld is an excellent, virtually untapped field for the collector.

The Banque de France continued to print paper money through the war years and up to the present. The twentieth century brought changes in its execution, however. First, partly as a result of the war, France experienced inflation, reflected in the fact that bills in higher denominations—up to five thousand francs—became more common. This inflation was modest compared to what was going on in Germany—or what had gone on in France itself in the age of assignats—but it

was bad enough. Furthermore, it may have been a factor in the weakening of French determination which led to the German victory and occupation of the country in 1940.

The second change in Banque de France notes was the introduction of multicolor printing for all denominations, a process achieved in the 1920s and 1930s. Designed as a protection against counterfeiting, it gave France some of the most artistic money the world has ever seen, and it rendered counterfeiting virtually impossible. The notes illustrated are typical, and one can also see a shift from purely allegorical representations to bits of local color (a Breton family on the 1949 twenty-franc note) to famous persons and national heroes (Voltaire on the new ten-franc bill). Much modern French currency is available at low prices, especially pre-1960 **34** material.

▲ Top: Banque de France, 20 francs, 1949; below: Banque de France, 10 francs, 1973.

Benelux

The history of paper money in the three countries collectively known as Benelux (Belgium, the Netherlands, and Luxembourg) does not go as far back as does that of France, but it has seen the production of some outstandingly beautiful and interesting currency.

Belgium's paper money dates from the separation of that country from the Netherlands, when it became an independent kingdom in 1830. Nineteenth-century Belgian notes are difficult to obtain in any condition, and it is not until just prior to World War I that Belgian paper becomes available to the average collector.

The authority issuing paper money at that time was the Banque Nationale de Belgique, and its productions followed a practice that originated with the country's coinage. Each note was printed in two languages: French and Flemish. Belgium is in fact composed of two peoples—Flemings, who speak a language akin to Dutch, and the French-speaking Walloons. Belgium's money recognizes this fact.

The kingdom fell to Germany in the opening phase of World War I, and a new banking agency was set up to provide the country with paper money, the Société Générale de Belgique. The rather plain-looking notes of this bank provided basic currency needs during the German occupation. There were also a number of notes printed by various cities and towns to provide small change.

With war's end, the Banque Nationale de Belgique resumed its production of paper money, and it has supplied national needs to the present. As we saw in France, Belgian issues have shifted from allegorical representations to local scenes and famous Belgians for their designs.

For many years, Dutch currency tended to favor simple designs with a minimum of artistic embellishments. This was especially true of the state notes (*muntibiljets* and *zilverbon*). The paper money printed by the National Bank (Nederlandsche Bank) was always something of an exception to this rule, however, and by the outbreak of World War II, the National Bank was producing highly original, artistic banknotes; the twenty-gulden issue of 1939 is a typical prod-

uct. Other notes of this period featured famous people from Holland's past and reproductions of paintings by Rembrandt and other great Dutch artists.

The Netherlands was fortunate enough to stay out of World War I; it was not so lucky twenty years later, and the country was occupied by the Nazis from 1940 to 1945. Paper money continued to be produced in Holland following prewar designs, but an interesting series of notes was also produced in the United States, presumably for use in Dutch possessions abroad, and hopefully in Holland itself after liberation. Postwar Dutch issues are outstanding for their simple, clean, innovative designs.

Luxembourg has produced paper money in fairly limited quantities. As with Belgian issues, Luxembourg notes are bilingual. Some of the earliest issues, dating from the 1850s, were the product of the Banque Internationale à Luxembourg; all are rare. Luxembourg was occupied by Germany during both world wars, and Germany provided the grand duchy with currency. This, too, is rare. Somewhat more common are the state notes of the grand duchy itself, portraying local scenes, current rulers, and the like. Designs have generally been conservative.

▲ *Left to right: Belgium. 500 francs, 1943; 50 francs, 1956; Bruges, 5 centimes, 1915. Top: Netherlands. 10 gulden, 1968; bottom: 20 gulden, 1939.* ▶

▲ *Luxembourg, 20 francs, 1929.*

Iberia

Spain and Portugal were indirectly responsible for the spread of paper money in Europe. When Spanish and Portuguese explorers discovered vast new sources of undreamed-of wealth in the Indies, they increased the total world monetary supply. Paper money was devised by foreign merchants as a way of handling this new-found wealth with greater convenience, so it is somewhat surprising that paper money did not become widespread in Spain and Portugal until late. This highlights one sad fact: most of the gold and silver found in the Americas did not stay in the two Iberian countries. Instead, it continued on to England, France, and the Low Countries as payment for manufactured goods. Northern Europeans got rich, while the Spanish and Portuguese remained poor. Poor people do not require much money of any kind.

Spain's first paper money dates from 1783, issues of the Banco Nacional de San Carlos. This bank—and other early, note-emitting Spanish banks—functioned with patents of privilege from Spain's rulers. All of them printed large-sized paper money in a single-color format. All of the banks had ceased to exist by the middle of the nineteenth century, and their notes are among the rarest of all paper money.

By the mid-1850s, a number of provincial banks were being set up in population centers such as Barcelona, Cádiz, and Malaga. Most of these banks were short-lived, and their notes, too, are very rare today. By this time, the major producer of Spanish paper money had come into being, the Banco de España. Formed in 1856, the Banco de España almost immediately achieved a position of dominance over the Spanish paper-money system, and the notes of this agency are those that the paper-money collector is most likely to come across.

Spain's paper money reflects the turbulent tide of the nation's economic and political history over the past hundred years. Spain is a nation proud of its past. Thus, it comes as no surprise to learn that a celebration of that past has always been a popular feature of Spanish paper money. A hundred-peseta note of 1925 shows Philip II, one of Spain's greatest rulers; a five-peseta note of 1945, a product of the Franco state, shows **38** Christopher Columbus and his patroness, Queen Isabella.

Illustrated are two curious examples of Spanish paper money, both of them dating from the time of the Spanish civil war (1936–39). First, a close look at the paper money printed for the Franco government shows that most of it was printed in Germany. When we consider the amount of German and Italian aid to the Nationalist (Franco) side in its attempt to overthrow the Spanish Republic, we can understand why there was German-printed paper money in Spain. It was simply another form of foreign aid. Also, the Spanish civil war saw the issue of a vast amount of emergency local paper currency by both sides in the conflict. Much of this material is still available to the collector, and it makes a good addition to any paper-money collection. The piece illustrated was made by republican forces in 1937.

▲ *Spain, Banco de España, 500 pesetas, 1971.*

▲ *Spanish civil war. Top: detail of Banco de España note printed in Germany, 25 pesetas, 1938; bottom: Almahade, one peseta, 1937.*

The earliest Portuguese paper money dates from the late eighteenth century, although it did not become widespread until the beginning of the twentieth. Its history generally parallels that of paper currency in Spain. Under the monarchy, which lasted until 1910, issues of the Banco de Portugal tended to follow a fairly simple design; since the establishment of the republic, a multicolor format and more ornate designs have been favored. An unusual feature of late nineteenth- and early twentieth-century Portuguese currency is that much of it was a product of the national mint, which printed bills in low denominations to circulate in place of minor coinage. This practice went on for more than thirty years, engendered in part by the country's economic difficulties at that time.

▲ *Portugal. Top: Banco de Portugal, 20 escudos,*
1964; bottom: Casa da Moeda, 10 centavos, 1917.

Italy

Italian paper money has found increasing favor with collectors due both to its availability and to its faithful reflection of the country's tumultuous political and economic history.

The first Italian paper money dates from the eighteenth century, and it bears accurate witness to the political chaos before the creation of a unified country. Kingdoms such as Savoy (the eventual architect of a united Italy) issued paper, much of it with an ornate design for those times. When the French invaded Italy and set up puppet republics, their governmental creations also printed paper money. One such note, a product of the short-lived Roman Republic, is illustrated. If anyone doubts the close ties Italy had with France, note that the date is given in accordance with the French Revolutionary calendar! These issues are occasionally encountered, although much less frequently than their French counterparts, the assignats.

A number of private banks came into being in the nineteenth century, many of them with note-printing privileges. The 1868 issue of the Banca del Popolo, a Florence concern, is typical both in terms of design and in terms of the condition in which these notes are ordinarily found. Though they are not particularly rare, the uncirculated specimens are scarce. It should be noted that the private banks continued to print paper money long after Italy's unification—the hundred-lire banknote from Naples dates from around 1920, and private notes continued to be issued until 1926.

Italy's unification under the House of Savoy in 1861 wrought great changes in the nation's paper-currency system. The Banca d'Italia was quickly set up, a national institution that has dominated Italian paper money ever since, issuing notes in lire denominations, the currency unit of the new nation. In addition, there have been *biglietti di stato,* state treasury notes, printed directly by the government.

Italy's paper money has reflected the rise and fall of political philosophies and regimes. The 1904 biglietto di stato illustrated, for instance, has Vittorio Emmanuele III firmly on his throne, the main vignette on the bill. The 1939 counterpart of **42** this note reflects a change in the national order. The king is still

represented, but so are *fasces*, the emblems of the real power in Italy at the time, the dictatorship of Benito Mussolini. An issue of the wartime fascist state dropped the king entirely: a close look shows two *fasces* at the right, the wolf-and-twins motif of Imperial Rome in the center (Mussolini was theoretically attempting to reestablish the ancient Roman Empire), and another *fasces* on the left with the date of the founding of the Italian dictatorship—October 1922. Incidentally, this note, a product of the Banca d'Italia, illustrates a rather annoying practice used on many Italian bills: no actual date of issue is given; instead, we are informed of the dates of all legislation relative to the issue of that particular bill. Taking the latest year represented and adding a year or two more should give a reasonably accurate date. In the case of this particular note, the dating is rendered somewhat easier by the fact that, when Mussolini was overthrown in 1943, the red *fasces* device was removed.

By now, Mussolini's dreams were in ruins. The Allies invaded Italy and issued occupation currency, as they would do later in Germany, Japan, and other countries. The notes in question were not paragons of the printers' art, but they circulated readily enough, forming an important part of the Italian economic system until war's end. The occupation notes were printed in denominations ranging from one to one thousand **45**

lire, and since many American and British servicemen brought them home after the war, none are particularly rare today.

The printing of paper money in a thousand-lire denomination points to a long-range problem of the Italian economy, that of inflation. A century ago, one thousand lire would have been a large sum of money (there were five lire to the dollar in those days); now it represents a trifle more than one dollar. There have been several causes behind this inflation, not the least of which have been the vast expenses incurred by Italian participation in two world wars. Inflation's effects after World War I helped to bring down the parliamentary government and to produce the Mussolini dictatorship. Inflation is still a problem for the Italian economy and government, and it still produces unrest. It has also brought forth new, higher-denomination banknotes by the Banca d'Italia, honoring great Italian artists and writers.

The endemic Italian inflation has had the effect of removing most coinage from circulation (Italian coins are issued in denominations ranging from one to five hundred lire). As a result, private banks and corporations all over Italy are issuing the Italian equivalent of notgeld: small-sized emergency paper money, generally worth two hundred lire or less. The piece illustrated is typical, an example of a brand-new collecting field that is just opening up. Telephone tokens, postage stamps, even toll tickets are also seeing circulation, but the notgeld seems most popular. This should remind us that one of the original functions of paper money was to take the place of **46** coinage in time of scarcity. This function is still being met.

▲ Top to bottom: *Allied currency for Italy, 10 lire, 1943;*
Banca d'Italia, 10,000 lire, 1962–66;
private small change note from Palermo, 150 lire, 1976.

The Balkan States

The nations known collectively as the Balkan States (Greece, Romania, Bulgaria, Yugoslavia, and Albania) were all part of the Turkish Empire until recent times. As a result, the history of paper money in these countries is a relatively short one, although it can provide the hobbyist with some attractive specimens for his or her collection. An interesting series of high-denomination currency was produced by Greece, when she experienced one of the most disastrous inflationary spirals in history.

The Greeks were the first Balkan people to throw off the yoke of Turkish control, and they also issued the earliest Balkan paper money. An early specimen note of the National Bank of Greece is illustrated. The note, dating from about 1860, was printed in New York, since Greece lacked the technology to print paper money at that time. The central vignette (two maidens) originally appeared on an American private banknote. It was transferred to a new plate to produce this bill, and an engraving of a Grecian temple was added to lend the note greater authenticity! Many nineteenth-century issues printed in the United States for other governments also employed retooled plates, and many paper-money collectors enjoy attempting to trace designs back to their original sources.

Most later Greek issues were products of the National Bank of Greece or its successor, the Bank of Greece. This includes the paper money of the years of the disastrous Greek inflation, coinciding with Germany's occupation of the country in the early 1940s. Greece's currency has always celebrated the national past with representations of great masterworks of sculpture and architecture—or coinage—as on the ten-thousand-drachmae note illustrated. Unlike most Balkan paper money, issues from Greece are plentiful, making an interesting field for the beginning or advanced collector.

Romanian issues are scarcer. Early Romanian notes were often printed in France. They closely resembled current French issues in the use of allegorical motifs and pastel, multicolor printing processes. Later issues of the Communist state have been home-produced. They feature a prominent display **47**

▲ Left: 25 drachmae, c. 1860; r: 1 drachma, 1885.

of the national arms and scenes that proclaim the country's wealth.

Bulgaria achieved its freedom from the Turkish empire in the late 1870s, and its subsequent political and economic history roughly paralleled that of Romania—a principality until the turn of the century, a kingdom after that, and a Communist state following World War II. There are differences between the two countries in the matter of their money, however. Bulgaria was in part a creation of the Russian Empire, and much of its early currency, printed in Russia, closely resembled that country's paper money. This similarity is made more manifest by the fact that Bulgarians use a Cyrillic script, resembling Russian. Later Bulgarian issues were usually printed in London, using fewer colors and less allegory than Romanian currency.

Like Romania, Bulgaria experienced serious inflation at the end of World War II. This inflation and the consequent unrest helped bring down the monarchies in both countries, leading **49**

to the establishment of Communist states. Bulgarian issues under the new regime have been quite attractive, with multicolored, florid but pleasing designs, designs that once again resemble contemporary Russian issues.

The paper-money history of Yugoslavia is complex. The Serbs and Montenegrins gained their independence from Turkey in the later nineteenth century. They issued currency in limited quantities, most of it printed in neighboring Austria, until the outbreak of World War I. The area emerged from that conflict with a new, collective nationality as the kingdom of Yugoslavia. Its notes, usually patterned after contemporary French issues, are occasionally encountered, as are those of the old Serbia, and less frequently, Montenegro.

World War II decimated Yugoslavia, ruined its economy, and eventually brought a new regime—the Communist state of Josip Broz (Tito). Modern Yugoslav paper money tends to depict typical local scenes and citizens of the six federative republics. Each note is multilingual, a scrupulous attempt to represent all of Yugoslavia's ethnic groups.

Albania was the last Balkan nation to free itself from Turkey, and its paper money is the least available to collectors. Some of the earlier notes of the kingdom of Albania bear legends in Italian as well as Albanian, for Italian influence was strong in this part of the Balkans. Modern issues of the postwar Communist state tend to resemble those of Bulgaria.

50

▲ *Top: Yugoslavia, 100 dinar,*
1963; bottom: Albania 5 franka ari, 1926.

Germany

German paper money has always been a favorite with collectors. There are literally thousands of types available, in both local and national issues. The famous German inflation notes lend additional attraction to this series, as do the many artistic designs employed on German currency. Best of all from the collector's standpoint, a great deal of Germany's paper currency is inexpensive, due to the sheer quantity still available.

The earliest German paper money dates from the 1700s, a product of the various kingdoms and principalities of the period. All of this material is rare. In addition, there were siege issues from time to time, especially during the Napoleonic Wars. The note illustrated is typical. It was printed by Prussian defenders of the city of Coburg, under siege by the French in 1807. It is similar to the earlier siege note we saw, which was printed in Mainz by French defending the town from the Prussians. Siege notes and other nineteenth-century examples of German paper are occasionally encountered, but none are especially common.

The major political development in nineteenth-century German history was the rise of Prussia. By 1871, Prussia had succeeded in welding a collection of free cities, principalities, and smaller kingdoms into a single polity—the German Empire. In theory, this was simply a federation of states of which the King of Prussia happened to be the head as Emperor of Germany. In practice, Germany was now a single country, with its capital in Prussia (Berlin) and with Prussian leadership.

All of this caused changes in Germany's paper-money system. There was now a standard national currency, the mark. And while the smaller kingdoms retained the right to print paper money, they gradually surrendered these rights to the Bank of Prussia, reorganized as the Imperial Bank (Reichsbank) in 1876. It was not until the early days of the Hitler regime, however, that the last state banks were suppressed. Collectors occasionally run across late nineteenth- and early twentieth-century examples of notes from state banks, but the condition of the notes generally leaves much to be desired. The vast majority of official German currency now available are products of the Reichsbank, which printed na- **51**

▲ *Top: siege note (Coburg), 1807; bottom: Prussia, 10 thaler, 1870.*

tional paper money through the Empire (to 1918), the Weimar Republic (1919–33), and the Third Reich (1933–45).

The issues of Imperial Germany are fairly common, and the hobbyist should have no trouble in assembling a representative collection at only moderate expense. All of the Reichsbank issues of this period are attractive, usually printed in one or two colors, in an ornate design. The reverses commonly employ allegorical figures—the spirits of Germany, of Commerce, Agriculture, etc. The thousand-mark note pictured is typical. Although dated 1910, it was printed towards the end of World War I, and the relative availability of this high-denomination bill is the first indication of the disastrous inflation that would soon engulf Germany.

The war saw the first appearance of one of the most common types of German paper money, notgeld. In 1914, people began hoarding ordinary coinage and paper money. The government tried to deal with the problem by printing a new type of paper, *Darlehenskassenscheine* (state loan notes), mainly in small denominations. Production failed to meet demand, however, and towns and cities, even factories and cooperatives, soon began printing paper for local use. This was notgeld.

Notgeld was produced all over Germany, both during and after the war. One can distinguish at least four categories: early, quite primitive issues of 1914; later, somewhat more elaborate printings of 1916–18; low-denomination, ornate productions of 1919–22; and high-value notes of 1922–23. Let us briefly examine each type.

The issues of 1914 and 1916–18 really were intended solely as a replacement for ordinary coinage and currency. This accounts for the primitive quality of the twenty-mark issues of Felleringen, a tiny village in the Upper Alsace. The authorities were not interested in producing a twenty-mark bill of outstanding beauty; indeed, had they wished to do so, a village so small was unlikely to have the necessary equipment. So they printed their notes from rubber type, stamped them with the Imperial eagle, and the *burgermeister* signed each—and the bills circulated perfectly well.

By the time of the second kind of bill, as illustrated by a 1918 **53** issue from Hamm, notgeld had become somewhat more sophisticated. This note was locally produced, but by this time many towns and cities were having their emergency currency produced in Berlin and elsewhere. A good deal of notgeld produced in the last months of World War I is available to the collector.

But the real explosion of types and varieties of notgeld took place after the war, from 1919–22. This third category of German emergency currency was generally issued in low denominations, one mark or under. When someone conceived the idea of collecting notgeld, the paper assumed a new purpose: not only would it serve a town's inhabitants in their

day-to-day transactions, but it would also be sold to tourists who had hard cash to spend.

So a notgeld boom began. Soon every town in Germany was producing it, whether they actually needed to or not. Better printing techniques were employed to print multicolored notes, intended to catch the collector's eye. Notebooks to hold notgeld were produced, and they, too, enjoyed brisk sales. This later notgeld pictured everything from local scenery to local heroes, from Germanic legends to doggerel poetry to propaganda. The message on the 1921 fifty pfennig from Hamburg was impossible to misinterpret—it showed a German soldier crucified on a sword, a reference to the Allies.

The final type of notgeld, dating from 1922–23, was a reflection of the inflation Germany was experiencing. Once again, this notgeld was basically designed for internal consumption, not for the collector, and it is much rarer than the 1919–22 material. The note illustrated comes from Bielefeld, today part of West Germany, and its inscriptions comment on the current inflation and cost of living.

As previously mentioned, Germany's inflation was a disaster for the country. Its roots lay in World War I, and by the time it had run its full course, the German middle class was in ruins. A pervading aura of cynicism was upon the land, a scorn for the ineffectiveness of democratic institutions in getting things done (for example, fighting inflation). This helped pave the way for the rise of Adolf Hitler.

56   We can see something of the frustration and chaos of the

▲ *Top: Bavaria, 5 billion mark, 1923;*
bottom: Weimar Republic, 20 reichsmark, 1929.

pre-Hitler years reflected in the national currency of the Weimar Republic. The early issues of the reconstituted Reichsbank proclaim the undiminished strength of the German people, an attempt to inject a note of optimism into the consciousness of a defeated nation. The note illustrated is a fifty-mark bill. It was a sizable amount of money when it was issued in 1920, but inflation would soon render it worthless.

Germany's hyperinflation got under way in 1921, when larger and larger notes were printed. A five-hundred-thousand-mark bill made its debut in May, 1923, and while printed in a denomination undreamed of before the war, it was still a handsomely designed, carefully printed piece of money.

▲ *Top to bottom: 50 mark, 1920; 500,000 mark, 1923; 5 million mark, 1923.*

But by late summer, all attempts to hold down inflation had failed, and the Reichsbank was circulating high-denomination notes as fast as it could print them. And it printed them in astronomical quantities: one reason why German inflationary currency appears crudely printed and designed is simply that so much of it was produced that there was insufficient time to prepare and execute decent designs. In any case, if a bill is likely to be worthless in two weeks, why bother?

In addition to federal issues, the component German states printed their own inflationary currency, and so did localities, as we have seen. Early in 1924, the German government was finally able to bring a halt to the hyperinflation. Large loans were secured from the United States, the national debt was repudiated, and a new currency system, guaranteed by real estate mortgage bonds (a muted echo of John Law's schemes and the French assignats), was introduced. Germany's currency would henceforth be stable. Her government was another matter.

Dissatisfaction with the Weimar Republic, never entirely silenced during the prosperous late 1920s, grew louder with the coming of the Great Depression. Once again, as in the case of the recent inflation, the government seemed powerless to act. As the depression deepened, as the republic had no clear plan to fight it, interest grew in a right-wing, highly nationalist movement called Nazism. Adolf Hitler, leader of the Nazi party, took power in the opening days of 1933, would hold it for the next twelve years. His Third Reich would produce permanent changes in Germany's political history and in her money.

Except for abolishing the last of the local, note-issuing banks in 1935, Hitler did not directly change the German currency system in any notable way. Germany's banknotes continued to resemble the 1929 issue illustrated, portraying famous people. But Germany's entry into World War II *did* alter German paper money. Germany lost the war, found herself occupied by Allied troops, and eventually became two nations, one Western-oriented, the other aligned with the USSR. And German currency reflected all these events.

58   When the Allies occupied the country, they printed paper

▲ German Federal Republic, 100 deutsche mark, 1960.

money on the Italian model, in values ranging from one to one thousand marks. These notes are widely available today, as returning servicemen often kept them as souvenirs. As the cold war set in, the division of the former Third Reich into temporary zones of Allied occupation deepened and grew permanent. The three Western zones became the German Federal Republic, or West Germany, and the Soviet zone metamorphosed into the German Democratic Republic, commonly called East Germany. Both halves of the formerly unified country have printed paper money, beginning in 1948. West German issues are probably more attractive, featuring works by German painters, and more plentiful than are the notes of East **60** Germany.

▲ German Democratic Republic, 50 mark, 1971.

Middle Europe

Middle Europe is a geographical concept embracing the old Austro-Hungarian Empire and its successor states (Austria, Hungary, Czechoslovakia, and Poland). Middle Europe offers a fertile field for the paper-money collector: notes of great historical interest and beauty, currency that bears testimony to the rise, fall, and rebirth of the Middle European states.

When paper money first appeared here, about the same time it came to Germany, Austria controlled most of Middle Europe. The Austrian Empire printed large amounts of paper currency in the late eighteenth and early nineteenth centuries. The note illustrated from 1800 is typical of this early currency. The use of a vertical format continued for many years, as can be seen on a note of the Austrian National Bank from 1858.

By the middle 1800s, the various nationalities comprising the Empire were chafing under Austrian rule. In 1848, full-scale revolt broke out against the monarchy, quickly spreading to all parts of the country. The scene of the worst fighting was Hungary.

Hungary had been part of the Austrian Empire for two centuries, but Hungarians were divided from their Austrian rulers by language, ways of life, and, to a degree, by religion. They never considered themselves part of a united Austria, and they detested rule by foreigners. Disturbances in other parts of the Austrian domains gave the Hungarians the courage and the opportunity to undertake a struggle for their own independence. Their leader was a radical politician named Lajos Kossuth.

This first Hungarian revolution was fairly bloodless in its initial stages. When the Austrian government managed to restore order in Vienna by the middle of 1848, they then undertook to quell the Hungarian unrest. Led by Kossuth, the Hungarians fought back heroically, but they were finally defeated in August, 1849, in part because the new Austrian Emperor, Franz Josef, obtained the services of a Russian army.

All of this is important for the paper-money collector because the Hungarian uprising produced two interesting series. The first was printed in Budapest during the actual rebellion, promissory notes guaranteeing payment in cash eight years **61** from the date of issue. The second series of Hungarian revolutionary paper is closely tied to the fortunes of Lajos Kossuth. Fleeing Hungary with the collapse of the uprising in mid-1849, Kossuth turned up in the United States two years later, attempting to gather support for a second revolution. He ordered a new issue of Hungarian paper money printed in the United States, presumably intending to take it with him to his homeland. He obtained the services of a well-known printer of American private banknotes, and a bizarre series of currency resulted, entirely printed in Hungarian by a group of Americans who could not speak a word of the language! Kossuth's American-printed revolutionary currency is still widely avail-

able, for the simple reason that he was never able to return to

▲ *Austria. Left: gulden, 1800; right, gulden, 1858.*
Hungary. Center: 30 krajczarra, 1849; background:
Kossuth bills printed in U.S.A., c. 1851. ▶

▲ Austria, krone, 1916.

Hungary and put his paper into circulation. He got a good deal of American sympathy, and the state of Iowa named a county after him, but if he expected an outraged America to free Hungary, he was sadly disillusioned. Kossuth died in 1894, still in exile.

The entire Hungarian episode did convince Austria that some sort of reform would have to be undertaken. What resulted was a dual monarchy, the Austro-Hungarian Empire. Franz Josef continued to rule as head of both the Austrian and the Hungarian states. But the Empire was now constitutionally divided into two parts, Austria controlling one half, Hungary the other. Except in matters of foreign policy, the Hungarians were now independent.

This did not apply to minorities (Poles, Slovaks, and many others) who lived under Hungarian rule, nor did it apply to **64** minorities living in the Austrian half of the Empire. These

▲ *Austria. Left: 20 schilling, 1956; right: 1,000 kronen, 1919–20.*

discontented peoples would eventually bring down the Austro-Hungarian state. The ethnic complexity of the situation is indicated by a korona note of the Austro-Hungarian Bank (the state-run banking institution), which bore information in ten different languages in an attempt to keep everyone happy. This bill dates from 1916, and by that time the multinational empire was fighting for its life in World War I.

Of all the participants in World War I, Austria-Hungary lost the most. The Russian tsar lost his life, but Russia remained. The German emperor lost his throne, but Germany remained. Austria-Hungary, however, disappeared from the map. One by one, her peoples simply announced that they were leaving the Empire, and then did so. Czechoslovakia and Poland emerged from the ruins as new states. Romania, Italy, and Serbia (now Yugoslavia) expanded at imperial expense. A new Austria and a new Hungary also came into being, both **65**

▲ *Hungary. Top: 100 pengo, 1930; bottom: 100 forint, 1968.*

shadows of their former selves.

The first postwar currency of the Austrian Republic was simply an overprint applied to previous issues of the monarchy. A period of rampant inflation was followed by a currency reform in 1924 and the introduction of a new monetary unit, based on the schilling. Austria's currency in the interwar years tended to rely heavily on allegorical figures for design inspiration. Most of these notes are not readily available to the collector, nor are they particularly attractive, in contrast to the overprinted notes and some of the inflationary ones.

Austria was occupied by Hitler's Third Reich in the spring of 1938, a prelude to World War II. Austria regained its independence after the war, and its clean-lined, multicolor paper currency, still based on the schilling standard, depicts the national arms and famous Austrians on the obverse, and often a local scene on the reverse. Modern Austrian paper is readily available to the collector.

The story of Hungarian paper money since 1918 is highlighted by the disastrous hyperinflation of 1945–46, which we have already discussed. The first issues, like those of Austria, were simply overprints on earlier imperial currency. Hungary's currency was reformed in 1925, and the new unit, called a pengo, remained stable for almost twenty years. Some beautiful notes were printed by the Hungarian National Bank (Magyar Nemzeti Bank), such as the hundred pengo of 1930. In 1946, the Hungarian currency system was completely

▲ Czechoslovakia, 1,000 korun, 1934 (specimen).

BANKOVKA STÁTNÍ BANKY
ČESKOSLOVENSKÉ
STO KORUN
ČESKOSLOVENSKÝCH
1961

rebuilt, the new monetary unit being called a forint, the name Kossuth had given to his Hungarian currency almost a century before. A new series of paper money was printed, honoring Kossuth himself and other national heroes. The general format of Hungarian currency has remained virtually unchanged since that time, except for the old coat of arms that has been replaced by that of the Communist state.

The history of Czechoslovakia's currency began with the country's creation in 1918. At first, the new nation used whatever it could find for paper money, including overprinted Austro-Hungarian currency. These emergency issues were quickly replaced by new, national paper money, printed in Czechoslovakia or the United States, one of the prime movers in the creation of the country.

By the 1930s, Czechoslovakia was printing some of the most beautiful paper money of the interwar period, multicolor masterpieces with allegorical figures, vignettes of famous men of letters, and delicate uncluttered designs. The 1934 one-thousand-korun note of the Czechoslovak National Bank is a typical product of these times. A close look will reveal that the denomination was printed in German. Ostensibly to help the German minority living in Czechoslovakia, Hitler occupied the country in 1938–39. Hitler set up two puppet states in the years following: Bohemia-Moravia and Slovakia. Their notes are occasionally encountered today. They were repudiated by the postwar Czech government. After the war, Czechoslovakia **67**

▲ *Czechoslovakia, 100 korun, 1961.*

soon became aligned with the Soviet Union as the Czechoslovak People's Republic. Its early issues tended to be fairly drab, but later products have been more attractive, often portraying peasants and workers, or glorifying Czech industry.

Prior to 1795, Poland was independent, and it issued its own paper money, most commonly in the form of assignats somewhat like the French. From 1795 to 1918, Poland was divided between Germany, Austria, and Russia. Poland's paper money reflects this tripartite occupation, each nation occasionally issuing currency for its part of Poland.

By 1918, Poland was free. Her early issues closely resemble Austrian ones; indeed, some of them may have been printed there. Poland soon started printing her own money, a process that was abruptly terminated in 1939, when Germany once more occupied the land. Poland emerged from the war as a People's Republic, tied closely to the Soviet Union. The prewar monetary system, based on the zloty, was reestablished. Early postwar issues are fairly drab; more modern ones are an improvement in design, with vignettes picturing Polish peasants, workers, and national heroes.

Scandinavia

European paper money originated in Scandinavia in the seventeenth century. Since that time, the currency of the four Scandinavian countries (Sweden, Denmark, Norway, and Iceland) has been marked by a great conservatism and infrequent changing of designs. Scandinavia has never issued paper money in large quantities, but its notes are well worth looking for, if only for their historical interest.

As discussed in the Introduction, the first European paper money came from Sweden. It was issued in 1661 by the Stockholm Bank of Sweden, and was followed by similar printings in 1662, 1663, and 1666. With the exception of this last issue, all of this early paper is excessively rare. It tended to follow the general format of a slightly later Swedish note illustrated here: as you can see, the design is simple to an extreme, and the bill is signed by several individuals as a guarantee of its legitimacy. However, this 1717 note was not a product of the Stockholm Bank, which had succumbed to the temptation of printing more paper than it could redeem and was abolished in the late 1660s.

Sweden continued to produce paper money in the eighteenth and nineteenth centuries, in part to unsnarl the national finances, which had become chaotic as a result of Sweden's wars with Russia and other large powers. By the time of the 1849 eight-schilling note, the country's finances were on firm footing. But her paper money had changed very little in appearance from the first issues.

By now, both private and state-run banks were printing paper money. All private banknotes were withdrawn from circulation after 1903, leaving the Royal Swedish Bank (Sveriges Riksbank) in control of all Swedish currency, a position it has retained ever since. Swedish paper became somewhat more elaborate than in earlier times, but designs were still simple compared to the rest of Europe, and there was virtually no change in them. A ten-kronor note of 1938 bears a design dating from 1892: a seated personification of Sweden, the value, and the date. The design would not only be continued until 1940 on the ten kronor, but all the way until the late 1950s on higher denominations.

69

◀ *Poland. Left: assignat, 5 zlotych, 1794; top right: 2 zlote, 1936; bottom right: 100 zlotych, 1976.*

Latest Swedish notes portray either the reigning monarch or earlier ones, such as Gustav Vasa, a prominent figure in the Reformation period. If previous policy is any indication, these designs are likely to be around for the foreseeable future.

Denmark's paper money does not go back as far as does Sweden's, although it does have a long history, as the 1804 rigsdaler note indicates. Danish currency tends to be somewhat less conservative than Swedish, the result being that there are more available types for the collector. Designs have also been more elaborate, both for earlier banknotes and for the issues of the present Danish currency authority, the Danish National Bank (Danmarks Nationalbank). Older paper printed by this organization frequently employed typical Danish scenes in their designs, along with elaborate tracery, adapted from medieval Danish sculpture. The five-hundred-kronor specimen note is a typical product of the National Bank during the late 1930s and early 1940s. The country was occupied by Germany from 1940–45, but this brought no basic changes in **70** Danish currency. It did produce an interesting set of occupa-

▲ *Sweden. Top: 10 kronor, 1938; bottom: 5 kroner, 1974.*

▲ *Denmark. Top to bottom: rigsdaler, 1804;*
25 øre, 1945 (for use by Danish troops in
Germany); 500 kroner, 1939 (specimen).

Top: Norway, 5 kroner, 1937; bottom: Iceland, 50 kronur, 1928.

tion currency, however, for use by Danish troops stationed in a defeated Germany after the war. These notes are much prized by collectors.

Norwegian and Icelandic paper money may be more briefly discussed, as issues have tended to be fairly sparse, and in neither country does paper currency have a long history. This is partly a reflection of political realities: Norway formed a part of Denmark, and later Sweden, until 1905; Iceland was Danish until 1944. Any paper money needed could frequently by supplied by the two mother countries.

Some Norwegian issues are known from the nineteenth century, but the bulk of the small amount of material available dates from after 1900. It has some similarities to Swedish currency: designs tend to be simple and not particularly attractive, although they change more often than their Swedish counterparts. The note illustrated is one of the better Norwegian productions, dating from shortly before World War II. The war and the German occupation brought no major changes to Norwegian currency.

Almost all Icelandic currency is rare, which is logical considering the country's small population. Bills are usually attractive, often portraying a famous person on the obverse, and a vignette depicting the dramatic Icelandic countryside on the

reverse.

The Baltic States

Finland, Latvia, Lithuania, and Estonia, collectively known as the Baltic States, have many similarities in language and religion. Their history presents parallels, too. All of them were occupied by foreign countries, the most important of which was Russia. They all achieved their independence at the time of the Russian Revolution in 1917. With the exception of Finland, all were reabsorbed by Russia after only a few decades of independence. For our purposes, these nations are of interest because they each printed paper money. Finnish currency is the easiest to obtain, but bills of the three short-lived smaller republics are also occasionally encountered.

Finland was a grand duchy of the Russian Empire from 1809 to 1917. This elevated status gave it many rights and privileges not seen in the rest of the sprawling Russian domains. Among these rights was that of issuing its own coins and paper currency. This it undertook in the later nineteenth century. From the first, Finnish paper money was distinguished by spare, almost modernistic designs and the use of a limited amount of colors—two or three at the most. Simply rendered allegorical motifs found favor. All of these generalizations are still true.

The Russian Revolution gave the Finns the opportunity to gain their freedom. The earliest paper money of the Finnish Republic was virtually identical to issues under the Russian Empire. The markkaa standard was retained, as were the format and designs of the bills, with one exception: an examination of the fifty-markkaa note illustrated shows a rosette design at top-center. This replaced the Russian eagle on earlier bills.

The use of allegory on later notes is shown by the five-thousand-markkaa issue of 1946, in which about a dozen nudes symbolize the agriculture and bounty of the Finnish land. This format appears on most bills of the period—the higher the denomination, the more nudes.

This large, allegorical type of paper money has been recently abandoned in favor of smaller-sized notes honoring various Finnish heroes and men of letters. The new bills are also more brightly colored than before. Most Finnish currency is moderately priced, considering its historical interest and fairly limited production.

The paper money of the other Baltic States is rarer. Freedom from the Russians was achieved in 1918 and lost again in 1940. Today the Baltic States form three of the constituent republics of the Soviet Union. All issued sparse amounts of currency, beginning in 1919 and abruptly ending with the 1940 occupation.

Latvia's issues are perhaps the most common, and many of them are fairly artistic. The twenty-five latu is typical of later Latvian productions; it was placed in circulation a scant two years before the end of independence. Latvia also produced some interesting notgeld during its first years as an independent country; the piece illustrated was printed by the Riga Soviet in 1919.

Lithuanian and Estonian paper money also appeared in 1919. Lithuanian paper tends to be drab; the national hero, Vytautas the Great, is shown on a good deal of it, including the 1922 note illustrated. Estonian currency was perhaps the most artistically designed paper money circulating in any of the three republics. There was heavy use of allegorical figures and typically costumed Estonian peasants, such as this farmer's wife, who appeared on notes issued from 1928 to 1940. Most Estonian paper money is scarce.

▲ Top: Finland, 50 markkaa, 1918; b: 500 markkaa, 1945.

▲ Top to bottom: Riga Soviet, 5 rubli, 1919;
Lithuania, litas, 1922; Estonia, 10 krooni, 1928.

Russia

The paper money of Russia offers an incredibly wide vista of collecting prospects to the hobbyist, wider than that of any other country in the world. It has everything: notes printed in beautiful colors and designs, notes of important historical significance, notes of high denomination, and notes that are low in cost. Small wonder that the currency of Russia is enjoying an upsurge in popularity at the present time.

It is convenient to categorize Russian paper money into three periods, though they do not necessarily coincide with Russian political history: Empire, from the mid-eighteenth century to 1917; Civil War, 1917–24; and Soviet State, 1924 to the present.

Russia's first-known paper money dates from 1769, during the reign of Catherine the Great, and issues appeared regularly under her successors, Paul I and Alexander I (1796–1825). These earliest Russian notes seem to be quite rare, and it is an historical fact that many of them were withdrawn from circulation by Tsar Nicholas I in 1841. The blue note illustrated dates from 1830, and it shows us what this early paper currency may have looked like. It is also typical of the condition in which most nineteenth-century bills are found: these notes circulated widely, and their state of preservation generally leaves much to be desired. Russian notes in crisp, unused condition are readily available to collectors, but almost all of them date from the last years of the empire.

Nicholas' decree not only recalled old Russian notes, but also created a new paper currency called "credit notes." The credit notes restored a measure of stability to Russia's paper-money system (Nicholas had called in earlier paper because there was too much of it in circulation, leading to inflation), but this stability was short-lived. Russia got into two wars, the Crimean (1854–56) and the Russo-Turkish (1877–78), and she paid for these contests by simply printing more paper money. The 1855 ten-ruble credit note is an early example. Notice the vertical format, which is a common feature of many Russian bills, both during the empire and afterwards.

The amount of paper money put into circulation by the
Tsarist government continued to grow as the years wore on.

Printing methods improved, and some outstanding examples of the engraver's art began to pour from the presses. The twenty-five-ruble note of 1909 is representative of later Tsarist currency. It is multicolored and ornate, featuring a portrait of the reactionary Tsar Alexander III (1881–94). Incidentally, a student plot against this ruler was put down in 1887, and the ringleaders were executed. One of them was a young firebrand named Ulyanov. Ulyanov had a younger brother, Vladimir Ilyich Ulyanov, who was very much impressed by the event. History knows him as Lenin.

In 1914, Russian mishandling of a political assassination in the far-off Balkans helped bring about World War I. As it became apparent that the war was not going to be over in a few months as all sides had hoped, the Russian government began issuing huge amounts of credit notes to pay for it. Inflation became a major problem for the tsar and his ministers, as people increasingly hoarded coinage, refused to accept paper money, and grew more and more discontented with imperial policies.

77

▲ *Five rubles; 1830.*

The hoarding of coinage was a major problem. Even low-value coins of one, three, and five kopek were withdrawn. To solve this part of the hoarding dilemma, postage-stamp currency was introduced in 1915. This new form of money was printed from plates originally intended for postage stamps. Issues were printed on thick paper so they would hold up in commerce. Instead of the reverse of these stamps being backed with glue, there were inscriptions showing the denomination and the reason for issuing stamps that were supposed to circulate as coins. These and other low-denomination issues are among the last paper money of the Russian Empire. They were turned out in vast quantities from 1915 to 1917 and are readily available to interested collectors today.

By early 1917, the imperial government was bankrupt. It was losing the war it had helped to begin. Industrial and agricultural production was off, helping to cause shortages of almost everything, including foodstuffs. Inflation was bad and growing worse. Perhaps most important, the peoples of the Russian Empire had simply lost faith in the competence of the **78** tsar. He could not win the war. He could not halt the shortages.

Postal currency, 3 kopeks, obverse and reverse, 1915–17. ▶

◀ *Left: 10 rubles, 1855; right: 25 rubles, 1909.*

He was becoming increasingly irrevelant to the daily life of the people. And when that happened, his overthrow was bound to occur.

The Russian Revolution began as a series of strikes and riots in Petrograd, the imperial capital. They grew into gigantic demonstrations against the monarchy and the war. When crack imperial troops went over to the side of the rioters, the end had come. Nicholas II was deposed in March, 1917. A provisional government was formed, one committed to keeping Russia in World War I. This was unwise since most Russians now wanted peace. The story of the rest of 1917 is the tale of the rise and triumph of a party that pledged to give the people what they wanted. Its name was the Social Democratic, or Bolshevik, party. Its leader was Lenin.

Through most of 1917, Aleksander Kerensky, leader of the provisional government, eyed Lenin and the Bolsheviks warily. Their popularity seemed to be growing daily, for they were promising the Russian people the three items they most desperately wanted: bread (an end to food shortages), land (the return of the land to the peasantry), and peace (an end to Russian participation in the war). Against promises like these, the provisional government could offer little. It was split on what the Russian future should be. Lenin's group knew exactly what it wanted. In November, the inevitable took place: there was a second coup, and Lenin took control in Petrograd and Moscow.

▼ "Babylonian" (multilingual Soviet note), 500 rubles, 1919.

Russia was now Communist…or was it? A civil war, perhaps the largest in history, raged for the next several years to determine who would rule. Lenin and the Communists eventually won, but it was by no means a foregone conclusion that they would. Consider the obstacles: the Bolsheviks controlled Moscow (which soon became the new capital) and Petrograd in the beginning. But most of the remainder of the country was in other hands, ruled by every faction from extreme right-wing monarchists to anarchist bandits who made Communists look tame by comparison.

Nor was that all. The Bolsheviks also had to contend with a virtual collapse in agriculture, industry, and communications, with bad harvests, and with a famine in the early 1920s in which several million people starved to death. **81**

▲ *Top: Odessa, 5 rubles, 1917; center: Odessa, 15 kopeks, 1917; bottom: Tomsk, 5 rubles, 1918.*

Moreover, most of the outside world looked on the Communist assumption of power with abhorrence, and several of the major powers decided to do something about it. A defeated German Empire kept its troops in much of Russia until the early 1920s, stirring up trouble. A multinational expeditionary force was put together in 1918, led by France and Great Britain, along with the United States, Japan, and several smaller countries. It invaded northern Russia and spent the next two years fighting Communists. Poland invaded Russia in the spring of 1920, and she was only repulsed with great difficulty. And the famous Czech Legion wandered from one end of Russia to the other, sowing discord wherever it went.

Finally, many minority groups within Russia itself saw the collapse of tsarist authority as a God-given opportunity to assert their own independence. Foremost among them were the Baltic peoples, the Ukrainians, and the inhabitants of Geor-

▲ *Mittau (Western Volunteer Army), 10 mark, 1919.*
Blank reverse used to print Latvian postage stamps in 1920.

gia, Armenia, and Azerbaijan, in southern Russia. These peoples would cooperate with whoever offered them help in the achievement of their national ideals.

The result of all this was a many-faceted conflict, combining the worst aspects of a civil war, a war for ideologies, and wars between nations. In its most active phase, it would last from 1917 until the end of 1920. And in its wake it would bring problems that would not be solved until 1924, the year of Lenin's death.

In its struggle to assume the authority vacated by the tsar, the Communist regime had two basic advantages: it was operating from a centralized base, which its enemies were not, and it had at least the tacit cooperation of a majority of the Russian people. The Tsarist monarchy had so discredited itself that its supporters (called "Whites" to distinguish them from the "Reds," or Communists) could not count on much help from the Russian people themselves. White armies marched and countermarched all over Russia, but they were operating in something of a vacuum. So Lenin's supporters won, and the world was changed forever.

These events have been described in some detail because **83**

▲ *Top: Northwest Front, 1,000 rubles, 1919;*
bottom: Provisional Government of Far East, 100 rubles, 1920.

they produced an incredible amount of paper money by virtually everyone involved in the conflict. A civil war is likely to produce fears for the future on the part of the people who are living through it. In such a circumstance, coinage disappears from circulation. But something has to be used to buy and sell things, and armies have to purchase supplies, feed troops, and so forth. Inevitably, Russians of all political faiths turned to the printing press. Literally thousands of types of paper money appeared, and they faithfully reflect the chaotic conditions of the times.

The paper money of the provisional government tended to be either reprints of Tsarist notes or fairly small-denomination currency, such as the forty-ruble note illustrated. Kerensky continued the Tsarist practice of printing postage-stamp money as well, but the imperial eagle was conspicuously absent on his issues. Later on, a distinctive one-thousand-ruble note was introduced, the reverse of which depicted the headquarters of the Duma (the Russian parliament), a reminder to the people that the provisional government had committed itself to popular representation.

When the Bolsheviks assumed power in Petrograd, they, too, reissued Tsarist currency for a time, but were soon printing notes of a more distinctive type. Significantly, many of them were of higher denominations than those previously seen: inflation had entered Russia's currency system and it would remain a grave problem until 1924.

One of the most interesting types of Bolshevik Civil War currency was produced in 1919. Its interest lies in the fact that each note bears the Marxist slogan ''Workers of the World, Unite'' in Russian, English, Italian, Arabic, French, German, and Chinese. Collectors often call these notes ''Babylonians,'' due to the multilingual text. When we consider that Russia was being invaded by several of the peoples whose languages appear, we may have a clue as to why this unusual format was employed—to sow dissension among foreign troops, most of whom had started out as workers.

By this time, hundreds of authorities all over Russia, both Red and White, were printing emergency currency to meet **84** their needs. On the Black Sea, the city of Odessa printed

postage-stamp money and more orthodox currency in 1917. In Siberia, a provisional White government in Tomsk printed a large amount of paper money the following year, when they were fighting the Soviets. In the Baltic region, a group of German freebooters printed their own paper money—in *marks*—late in 1919. When their armies were defeated, a good deal of their currency remained. The new Latvian Republic recycled it, printing postage stamps on the other side!

Some of the most plentiful White currency comes from south Russia. Here, two erstwhile Tsarist generals held sway from 1918 until early 1920, and they issued a very attractive series of large bills, most of them prominently displaying the Russian eagle and allegorical figures. On the eastern rim of Siberia, the provisional government of the Far East released a very distinctive set of bills—printed by the American Bank Note Company! They had been ordered by Kerensky, but had arrived too late. They were then transhipped to Eastern Siberia and used there.

As was mentioned earlier, several subject peoples on the edges of the old empire took advantage of the 1917 revolution **85**

▲ Top: Ukraine, 1,000 karbovantisv,
1918; bottom: Armenia, 1,000 rubles, 1920.

to make their bids for independence. Among them were the Ukrainians, three peoples in the Caucasus region, and several Baltic nationalities. The only ones who achieved permanent independence were the Finns, although Latvia, Lithuania, and Estonia also enjoyed several years of freedom. Elsewhere, the Ukranians, Armenians, Georgians, and Azerbaijanis were not so successful. Independent states were established in all of these areas, lasted only a few years, and then disappeared as the fledgling Soviet government became strong enough to reestablish control. All of these would-be nations printed paper money of varying degrees of sophistication; much of it employed allegories of a nationalistic type, and virtually all of **86** it is easily available to the interested collector.

▲ *Top: Georgia, 50 rubles, 1919; bottom: Azerbaijan, 5 million rubles, 1923.*

In a time of emergency, some unusual currency is apt to appear, and this was certainly true in Russia during the civil war. Towns like Odessa printed ordinary currency, but in a time of shortage, municipal bonds were also pressed into service as money. So were tramway tickets, meal coupons—anything, in short, with a recognized value. Nonofficial issues of paper money were also produced, such as notes from factories and cooperatives. One of the strangest is a 1918 three-ruble note, a product of the Kazan Gunpowder Works.

By 1920, the shooting phase of the Russian civil war had essentially ended. The Whites were on the run or had been crushed entirely, and the invading foreign armies were returning home. Lenin had triumphed. Russia was Communist. But **87**

▲ *Top right: Kazan Gunpowder Works, 3 rubles, 1918; center and bottom: Pskov Municipal bond, 40 rubles, 1918 and coupons, used as money.*

▲ *USSR, 100 rubles, 1947.*

▲ *Early issues of the Soviet Union. Top: 15,000 rubles, 1923; center: 50 kopeks, 1923; bottom: 3 rubles, 1925.*

the problems of the peace were to prove as defiant of a solution as the problems of the war. The country was devastated. Much of it had actually passed out of Russian control. Famine stalked the land. And inflation, a legacy from the war period, was growing worse and worse.

Inflation in Russia never reached the heights of absurdity that it achieved in Germany or Hungary, but when a nation prints a bill for fifteen thousand rubles, it is obvious that something is wrong. The Soviet state made several attempts to deal with the problem of inflation, but it was not until a measure of healing had been achieved by the land itself that a permanent solution could be found. A new, strong ruble was introduced in late 1923. Since no actual coins were being produced, an early product of the reform, a fifty-kopek note, was simply printed to *look* like one. State treasury notes were reintroduced in 1924–25, along with small change bills, which were retired as the Russians began producing the appropriate coins.

Soviet currency since 1924 has undergone periodic revaluations and stresses, but nothing like those it suffered during the civil war. Bills are very attractive, employing designs as ornate as any used on Tsarist paper money. Besides symbolic portraits of workers and peasants, Lenin is a favorite subject for Soviet notes, as are the national arms. In many ways, Soviet paper money closely resembles Tsarist, despite the great changes in the country since 1917.

89

▲ *Modern Russian paper. Left: 10
rubles, 1947; right: 25 rubles, 1961.*

Turkey and the Middle East

The paper money of Turkey and its former domains offer a fascinating, virtually untouched area of collecting possibilities. Prices are still low for much of this material, and the currency itself is historically interesting, and often quite artistic.

Turkey held sway over most of the region until after World War I. She began producing paper money for her dominions in the middle of the nineteenth century. While some of it was home-produced, other issues were printed abroad, in the United States. The 1861 note illustrated is a Turkish product, and it is fairly typical of nineteenth-century issues.

It should be mentioned that since the Moslem world uses a different numbering and dating system than does the West, the beginner may have trouble deciphering dates on Islamic currency. The Moslem calendar begins in 622 A.D., and their year is three percent shorter than the Christian year. This may be a trifle confusing, but for that reason it has served to keep prices low. The Appendix will show you how to go about finding the date and denomination of currency using this system.

The Turkish Empire put increasing amounts of paper money into circulation through the late nineteenth and early twentieth centuries. The government was almost always in debt, and it resorted to the printing presses to make up the difference. This led to a good deal of inflation and to periodic devaluation of the currency.

In 1915, Turkey went to war on the side of the Central Powers (Germany and Austria-Hungary). This led to widespread printing of unsupported paper money, which is still available in excellent condition. It also led to the dismemberment of the Turkish Empire, for the Central Powers lost World War I. New French- and British-administered states were set up in lands formerly ruled by the Turks. In Turkey itself, the changes were equally momentous. The monarchy had become completely discredited, and the last caliph, Mehmet VI, was overthrown in 1923. A republic was proclaimed. Its leader was one of the most extraordinary men of modern times, Kemel Atatürk.

Atatürk was a soldier by trade, a dedicated nationalist by

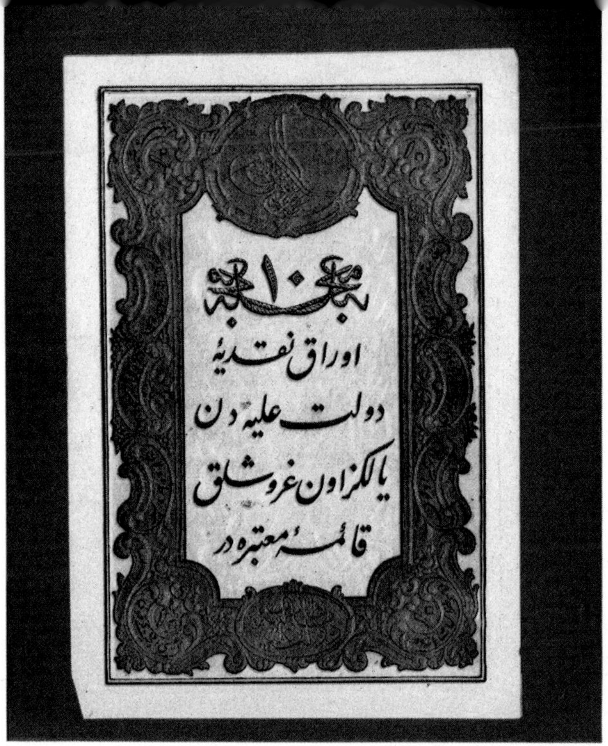

inclination. He realized that the Turkish Empire was dead, and that only if Turkey modernized could she herself avoid partition by larger countries. As dictator of Turkey from 1923 until his death in 1938, he sought, and largely achieved, a top-to-bottom modernization of the country and its institutions.

Turkish paper money reflects these changes. The difficult Turkish script was replaced by a new, Western-based alphabet. Arabic numbers were dropped in favor of Western ones, and the Moslem dating system was also abandoned. The old, confusing Turkish monetary system was replaced by a decimal one, based on the lira. Many of Atatürk's reforms were not fully accomplished in his lifetime, but he has been given full credit for them. He has appeared on most Turkish paper money from the 1920s to the present. Modern Turkish notes are quite attractive, employing a multicolored format and Atatürk's portrait on the obverse, a local landmark on the reverse.

91

▲ *Turkey, 10 ghrush, 1861.*

When Turkey was defeated in World War I, its empire was carved up into "mandates"—areas held by Britain or France, with the promise of eventual independence. Areas under British control included Palestine, Iraq, and Jordan. The French held Syria and Lebanon. Most of these mandates had their own currency, and after they were granted independence they continued to print paper money.

For Palestine, Great Britain produced an impressive series of trilingual bills in a scrupulous attempt to satisfy all of the inhabitants, Moslem as well as Jewish. The creation of the Israeli state in 1948 meant the continuation of paper-money production. At first, the new, made-in-Israel notes were quite crude, but later issues have been much more sophisticated, employing clean, modernistic designs and vignettes.

British paper for their mandate in Iraq was usually bilingual, featuring a portrait of the native head of state. More modern issues have dropped the ruler's portrait in favor of scenes of oil **92** production and national arms and building projects.

▲ Left: 5 piastres, 1916; top right: 5 lirasi, 1930; bottom right: 100 lirasi, 1970.

Neighboring Jordan did not have paper money of its own during its years as a British mandate. Its first currency was produced in 1949, after it became independent. Since then, all issues have pictured the king, along with a local scene and a text in Arabic.

The paper money printed by France for her mandates in Syria and Lebanon had French and Arabic inscriptions. The pastel, multicolor format employed on French banknotes was also used here. Currency of independent Syria has been less colorful, with vignettes of workers and peasants.

Lebanon's issues roughly paralleled those of Syria during the French mandate period, although there was less resemblance to French currency and more to contemporary Turkish and Palestinian (many of the notes were printed in England, and they were bicolored). Modern issues have depicted ancient ruins, such as the well-known city of Baalbek. Inscriptions are still in Arabic and French.

▲ Top: Israel, 5 lirot,
1973; bottom: Palestine, pound, 1929.

▲ Top: Iraq, dinar, c. 1935; bottom: Lebanon, livre, 1971.

Two countries of the Middle East, Iran and Afghanistan, were fortunate enough to retain their independence throughout the Turkish and mandate periods. Iran has been printing paper money since the nineteenth century, and while early issues are quite scarce, many of the more modern ones are not. Inscriptions are in Persian, except for the name of the issuing authority, which is often in English as well. Afghani notes resemble Iranian ones in design and degree of availability. The **94** distinctive coat of arms makes identification easy.

▲ Top: Iran, 10 rials, 1937–38;
bottom: Afghanistan, 50 afghanis, 1936.

Africa

Throughout the vast African continent, paper money is a recent development, coinciding with the beginning of European colonization there. That being the case, our discussion of African paper money will be based on the various colonizing powers and their independent successor states.

The Portuguese were the first Europeans to arrive on the scene. They did so in the fifteenth century, and they were soon striking coins for Angola, Moçambique, and Portuguese Guinea. Paper money was a much later development, and the earliest collectible notes from any of the colonies date from around 1900. They were produced in Lisbon by the Banco Nacional Ultramarino, and they are all identical except for the name of the specific colony, overprinted on the front and back of each bill. In addition, the largest colony, Angola, had a note-printing bank of its own. Banco de Angola currency exists from 1927 until the colony's independence almost fifty years later. A reflection of their independence, the new nations of Angola, Moçambique, and Guinea-Bissau are now setting up their own currency systems.

Next to arrive were the French. France appeared in North Africa in the early nineteenth century, and she began colonizing the central part of the continent about fifty years later. By 1910, in terms of sheer size, France's domains were the largest of any European country, although British holdings were more valuable.

Paper money faithfully reflected the path of French conquests. It closely resembled issues from the homeland. For example, the 1917 five-franc note of the Banque de l'Algérie looks like a contemporary French issue with the exception of a single line of Arabic script. Multicolored notes were introduced in French Africa about the same time they were in France, and most inscriptions were in the French language; denominations were given in francs. About the only differences between French and French-colonial paper were the themes portrayed: the currency of French African colonies is a rich source for pictures of the daily life of the native populations of the colonies.

Virtually all of the former French colonies are now indepen- **95**

▼ Top: Comoro Islands, 5,000 francs, 1976 (specimen); bottom: Morocco, 5 dirhams, 1970.

dent nations. Many of them, such as the Comoro Islands, have continued to rely on France to print their currency, and the paper money of these new states is among the most beautiful in the world. Other new nations, such as Morocco, have abandoned any ties with the former mother country, and their paper money reflects this fact, in format and inscriptions.

Tiny Belgium colonized the Congo from about 1885 on. Its currency for the Congo Free State (later known as Belgian Congo), closely copied homeland issues. Each bill was bilingual (although it's doubtful that the native peoples could read Flemish), and denominations were expressed in Belgian francs. All issues of the Belgian Congo are scarce to rare, as are those of Zaire, the name adopted by the former colony after independence.

The Germans came to Africa at about the same time as the Belgians. Their hegemony did not last as long, however. Germany lost her colonies of German East Africa, Togoland, and German South-West Africa during or immediately after World War I. The former German territories became Allied mandates. With the exception of South-West Africa, all are now independent nations.

While Germany's African venture was relatively brief, it did **96** result in the production of paper money for two of the col-

Top: Belgian Congo, 100 francs, 1927; center: German East Africa, 100 rupien, 1905; right: German East Africa, 5 rupien, 1917 (locally produced). ▶

onies, German South-West Africa and German East Africa. Prior to the outbreak of war in 1914, German South-West Africa used ordinary German currency. The war closed the normal channels of commerce, however, so colonial authorities printed notes of their own until 1918. All are primitive and rare. Issues are somewhat more plentiful for German East Africa. In Dar es Salaam, the Deutsch-Ostafrikanische Bank circulated bills in multiples of the rupee, the most widely used coin in the area. Early notes were printed in Germany, and they are fairly elaborate. The colony was cut off from the homeland at the outbreak of the war, and more primitive locally produced paper money was in use until 1918, one of the few examples of early African paper currency actually printed in Africa. These notes are more common than issues printed in Germany, and they're well worth looking out for.

The richest African colonial domain went to the British, who actually got into the colonial scramble fairly late. They moved rapidly, however; by 1905, they were masters of territory stretching from Cairo to the Cape of Good Hope. They printed paper currency for use in their new colonies. It was based on the British monetary system, and the Southern Rhodesian note in the illustration gives us an idea as to its appearance. By the early 1960s, most former British colonies had been granted their freedom. Many of their new, national issues closely resemble colonial ones in terms of overall design and monetary systems.

▲ Top: Southern Rhodesia, pound, 1938; bot: Kenya, 20 shillingi, 1975.
South Africa. Top: 2 rand, 1973; bot: pound, 1938. ▶

South Africa is something of an exception to this general state of affairs. Much of the country was settled by the Dutch, and the area became a British dominion in 1910. As such, it issued bilingual currency on a par with the British pound. The 1938 pound is representative of earlier South African issues. On close examination, one can see that the entire history of the country is reproduced in the large vignette, moving from left to right. South Africa became a republic in 1961, and its currency subsequent to that date has been based on the rand. Jan Van Riebeeck, who founded South Africa in 1652, is on each note.

The Indian Subcontinent

The history of paper money in the Indian Subcontinent (India, Pakistan, Bangladesh, Burma, Nepal, Bhutan, Sri Lanka, and the Maldive Islands) is influenced by the fact that all of these countries were at one time either part of the British Empire or indirectly controlled by it. In most cases, the English introduced the first paper money the area had ever seen. As these former portions of the British domain were granted independence, they continued to print paper money as a matter of financial convenience and a way of spurring the development of new nations.

The paper money of British India may be divided into two categories. In places where a semblance of native control was retained, state banknotes were issued. Many of them were locally produced and were often quite primitive in appearance. Others were printed in England, and they were as well designed as anything the British themselves were producing. Unfortunately most of these notes are quite rare. Notes in the second category—issues printed by the British for circulation throughout India––are much more numerous. The early notes bore simple designs, somewhat like their English counterparts. Later bills were more ornate, ordinarily portraying the reigning English sovereign (who was Emperor of India) and showing the denomination in the languages of the various ethnic groups comprising the country. This basic format was retained after India's independence, with the Ashoka Column, symbol of her freedom, replacing the portrait of the British monarch. Most Indian issues do not bear dates, and they tend to be less colorful than the paper money of some of the other nations in the area. India now prints her own money.

Three states, not one, resulted when India attained her independence in 1947. Most of India was Hindu, but there were many followers of Islam on the eastern and western fringes of the country. Independence for the newly created nation of Pakistan came in 1947. Burma, which had been administered by British India, also became free the following year. Late in 1971, yet another new nation was born, Bangladesh, formerly known as East Pakistan. These countries **100** have relied on paper currency since their independence.

Clockwise from top: Bangladesh, taka, 1972;
British India, 10 rupees, c. 1940; Republic of
India, 10 rupees, c. 1965; Pakistan, rupee, 1973. ▶

Ceylon, too, was a British domain until after World War II. Her paper money dates from about the same period as British issues for India; that is, from about the turn of the century. Ceylon became independent at the same time as India. In 1972, Ceylon changed its name to Sri Lanka, although much of the currency in circulation continues to bear the former name of the country. Sri Lanka's notes are usually multicolored, as are those of the Maldive Islands, a small nation off the Indian coast which became independent in 1965. The paper money of both Sri Lanka and the Maldive Islands depict native themes.

Far to the north lie the Himalayan states of Nepal and Bhutan, both of which have recently joined the world trend toward paper money. Nepal's notes feature a vignette of the reigning monarch and local scenery, including the Himalayas themselves. Bhutan's paper money features vivid colors, the ruler's portrait, and famous landmarks. Both nations have their **102** currency printed in neighboring India.

▲ *Left: Nepal, 5 rupees, 1956; right: Bhutan, 10 ngultrums, c. 1975.*

The Far East

The currency history of the Far East is a complex and fascinating one. As we have seen, the Chinese and Japanese were the earliest peoples to use paper money, and the majority of paper used in the Orient has come from these two nations. The collector also has a choice of materials from several other countries in the region, however, including Korea, Vietnam, and Thailand. Far Eastern currency represents some of the great bargains on the collecting market today, as many hobbyists are discovering.

The earliest Chinese paper money was the large-sized type illustrated on page 9. Depreciation of these notes led to abandonment of paper as a medium of exchange in China, and it was not until the mid-nineteenth century that this form of money was reintroduced, on the heels of European penetration of the Chinese Empire. The foreigners established a number of banks on the coast, and they were soon issuing paper currency. The Chinese themselves then followed suit, and by the late nineteenth century, there were a large number of note-issuing institutions, both European and native. One of the Chinese issues is illustrated here. It dates from around 1880, and it is a fascinating meeting of East and West. The green part of the note depicts Chinese scholars in traditional costume; the red depicts the Chinese impression of one of the new European trains that were opening up the country.

As time went on, Chinese banks began issuing bills which, except for Chinese inscriptions, were thoroughly European in format. The notes were generally bilingual: basic information in Chinese appeared on one side, English on the other. The first of these Occidental-appearing Chinese banknotes came out shortly before 1900, and they continued to be issued for the next fifty years.

In 1911, the Manchu dynasty was overthrown and the Chinese Empire became the Republic of China. The republican leader was a liberal lawyer, Dr. Sun Yat-Sen, and his portrait soon appeared on a great many Chinese bills. The coming of the republic complicated the paper-money history of China, however, for the republicans were unable to bring all of China under their control. They were opposed by various **103**

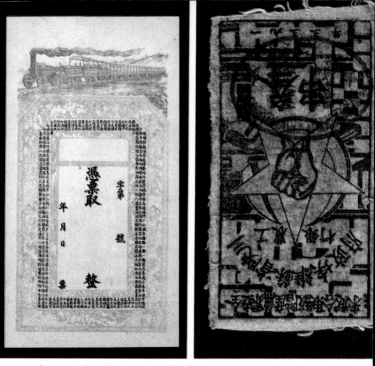

domestic leaders (the Warlords, among others), who were encouraged by foreign interests. This resulted in a rash of paper currency issued by Warlords, various state leaders, and private banks. It also resulted in a growing inflation.

China was finally unified by General Chiang Kai-Shek in the early 1930s. But a faction of Communists, led by Mao Tse-tung, continued to stir up trouble. Then, in 1931 Japan invaded the country. All these events are reflected in China's paper money. The Japanese set up banks in Manchuria and elsewhere as they expanded their political control. The Central and Federal Reserve banks of China were the primary banking institutions in the Japanese zone. Their notes are plentiful, as are those of the Bank of China and other republican fiscal authorities, the latter printing vast amounts of paper money to finance China's defense against Japan. Mao's group printed money, too, much of it on cloth (presumably because of greater durability).

▲ *Left: China, unfinished private banknote, c. 1880; r: Communist Chinese cloth note, 3 strings cash, 1933.*

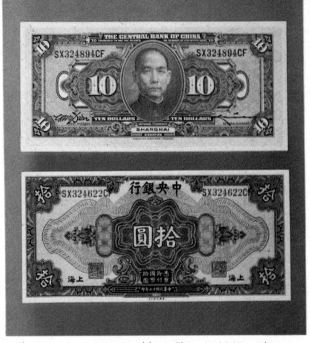

The Japanese were evicted from China in 1945, and matters now came down to a struggle for power between Chiang and Mao. By late 1949, the Communists controlled the Mainland, and Chiang's people found themselves in exile on Taiwan. So there have been two Chinas ever since, and both of them have issued paper money. Taiwan notes of the type illustrated are easier to find than are those of Mainland China, but the latter do appear occasionally. Both nations employ the yuan, or dollar, as their unit of currency.

Japanese issues are more scarce. Early Japanese currency was printed with wood blocks; the 1731 ten-momme gin note pictured is a sophisticated example of this process. These long, narrow bills were printed by both private and public authorities, and they form the typical Japanese paper money in use until the late nineteenth century.

In 1867, a new Japanese emperor, Meiji, came to the throne. For three centuries prior to this time, effective power had been **105**

▲ Top: Central Bank of China,
  10 dollars, obverse and reverse, 1928.

Top: North Korea, 100 won, 1947;
bottom: Thailand, 10 baht, 1969. ▶
▼ Japan. Left: 10 momme gin, 1731; r: 500 yen, c. 1965.

in the hands of the *shogun* (a sort of military dictator) and clan leaders scattered across the islands. Meiji brought an end to this feudal system, and beginning in about 1870 he made an all-out effort to modernize the country.

His accomplishments included the reformation of the Japanese monetary system. The yen was adopted as the nationwide unit of exchange, and the imperial government began placing modern treasury notes in circulation. Their first issues were printed abroad. By the 1880s, however, Japan was printing her own paper money, one indication that Meiji's modernization program was working. In the mid-1880s, the Bank of Japan (Nippon-Ginko) had been established; this institution is currently responsible for the production of all Japanese paper money.

In modernizing the country, Meiji had ulterior motives: a revitalized Japan would be able to play a larger role in world affairs and be able to expand her control to the Asian mainland. Japan warred with China in the mid-1890s, and with Russia ten years later. She won both contests, acquiring Taiwan and rights in Manchuria in the process. She absorbed Korea in 1910, and in 1931 invaded China.

All of Japan's efforts produced a strain on the currency. The value of the Japanese yen began to decline early in the twentieth century and continued to slip as time went on. At present, it takes approximately three hundred yen to purchase a United States dollar. A century ago, the two currencies were of equal value.

Japan's plans of conquest brought the nation's defeat in World War II. By 1945, the islands were devastated, and an American occupation force held command. It printed small, simply designed notes for Japan, just as it was doing for Germany and Italy. Since the end of the occupation, Japan has printed her own banknotes, in denominations ranging up to ten thousand yen. Japanese patriots and statesmen dominate the faces, and the beloved Mount Fuji is frequently portrayed on the reverse.

Like China and Japan, Korea was an early printer of paper money, but collectible Korean currency dates from the Japanese occupation and subsequent regimes. Both North and South Korea have produced paper money since their independence in 1945. North Korean notes, the rarer of the two series, employ a symbolic vignette of a worker and a peasant, or, later, a picture of a fishing boat and the national arms. South Korean issues have been more varied, depicting the country's first president, Dr. Syngman Rhee, on early notes, and national scenes and landmarks on later ones.

Thailand's paper money came as a result of European penetration of the country in the late nineteenth century. Foreign banks established note-issuing branches in Thailand from about 1890 to 1900. The Thai government established a **107**

◀ *Top: Taiwan, 10 yuan, 1969; bottom:*
People's Republic of China, yuan, 1953.

monopoly on circulating paper money in 1902, and it has held this position ever since. Most notes have been produced by the Ministry of Finance, including the one illustrated. The ruling monarch is usually portrayed on the obverse, a temple or palace on the reverse. The faint line running through this note is called a "security thread," and it is an innovation many nations have recently adopted as further protection against counterfeiting.

Indochinese paper money began with French occupation of this area in the 1880s, the first notes appearing in 1900. As with other French possessions, Indochinese currency was printed in France, and it closely resembled contemporary French issues in general format and choice of colors.

During World War II, Indochina was occupied by Japan. After the war, the French regained control, but found that a Communist guerrilla movement—originally against the Japanese, now turned against the French—became so costly to put down that they left the area. Four new nations emerged: North Vietnam, South Vietnam, Laos, and Cambodia. By 1976, all had become Communist states. These nations have issued some interesting currency, such as the multicolored Laotian note, still in circulation. The red and brown bill is a copy of a North Vietnamese dong, which the Americans counterfeited, adding a bit of anti-Communist propaganda on **108** the left side.

▲ Top to bottom: French Indochina, 20 piastres, c. 1950; Laos, 600 kip, c. 1970; U.S.A. counterfeit of North Vietnamese note (with propaganda message), c. 1972.

Oceania

The currency of the islands making up Oceania (the Philippines, Australia, New Zealand, Indonesia, and many smaller territories) make worthy additions to any paper-money collection. Some of the features of this currency are great historical value, outstanding beauty, and scenes of exotic peoples and customs. Most currency from Oceania is reasonably inexpensive, so that collecting possibilities are wide.

Paper money is a recent development in Oceania. Some of the earliest notes come from the Philippines; issues are known from the mid-1890s, but these and later nineteenth-century productions are quite rare.

The Philippines were a prize of the Spanish-American War, the United States occupying the archipelago in 1898, finally relinquishing control in 1946. The currency issued by the Philippines during these years graphically reflects the march of historical events.

Various banks and governmental organizations printed some paper money for island use from 1903 to 1941. This currency closely resembles contemporary American issues in basic format and choice of colors. The 1903 five-peso note illustrated is the Philippine counterpart to an American silver certificate. The gentleman on the left is President McKinley, during whose tenure the islands became a U.S. possession.

Things changed drastically late in 1941. In a lightning attack, Japan occupied the Philippines, and she was not evicted until early in 1945. Japan had notes printed for her new colony; most notes resembled the five-hundred-peso denomination illustrated. Incidentally, the letter P in red was a Japanese code to indicate that this note was intended for use in the Philippines. Similar issues were printed with a B for Burma, an O for Oceania, an M for Malaya, and an S for Indonesia.

Many Filipinos did not accept the Japanese occupation—or its money—and a constant guerrilla war enveloped the Philippines from the beginning to the end of Japanese rule. This led to an amazing series of notes printed by the guerrillas themselves, notes which circulated widely despite Japanese decrees threatening the death penalty for anyone found with them in their possession. The bill illustrated is one of the most **109**

▼ *Australia. Top: 10 shillings, 1939; bottom: dollar, c. 1970.*

◄ Philippines. Top to bottom: 5 pesos, 1903; 500 pesos, 1942; 10 pesos (guerrilla issue), 1942; 100 piso, 1973.

well designed. It comes from Leyte Province, which would later be the scene of one of the largest battles in the Pacific theater during World War II. Issues from more remote provinces were far cruder, sometimes merely mimeographs. Whatever the degree of sophistication, this emergency currency reflects the heroism of a people during a time of national crisis. Philippine emergency money is still available for moderate prices.

On July 4, 1946, the islands became the independent Republic of the Philippines. Modern issues of the Central Bank are colorful and well designed. They bear inscriptions in Tagalog, the official language of the new country, and they depict heroes of the country's struggle for independence.

Australian paper currency dates from the early part of the nineteenth century, although it is not available to the collector until much later. Early issues were products of private banks and businesses, and their numbers increased as the economy of Australia grew, due in part to the discovery of gold in 1851.

By the turn of the century, Australia had a new form of government—the Commonwealth. This new body took over the printing of Australian paper money, and it has fulfilled this **111**

▲ Top: Tonga, 4 shillings, 1955; bottom: New Zealand, dollar, 1967.

role for the last seventy-five years. Until 1966, Australian currency was based on the British pound. In that year, however, the country went on a decimal system, as the British themselves were to do a few years later. Now, the monetary unit in Australia is a dollar. The new, exceedingly well-designed Australian currency reflects the change from the pound to the dollar.

The history of New Zealand's paper money closely parallels that of Australia, including the adoption of a decimal system. New Zealand's currency designs emphasize native peoples, flora, and fauna to a greater degree than their Australian counterparts.

Many other islands in the British orbit have printed paper money at one time or another. Among the most interesting issues are those of Tonga, an independent island nation of the South Pacific. Earlier issues are in shilling denominations; since 1967, Tonga, too, has had a decimal currency, circulating at par with the Australian dollar.

The French have also printed paper money for their ter-

Indonesia, 100 rupiah, 1959. ▶

ritories in Oceania, such as Tahiti, New Hebrides, and New Caledonia. Notes now in circulation are multicolored, and they are among the most beautiful of any currency presently being produced. Some examples of typical vignettes are island scenes and peoples and famous French explorers of the area. Native motifs are used to frame the central vignettes on these handsome notes, many of which are quite within the financial reach of the collector.

Indonesia has also produced currency of outstanding artistry. The country was under Dutch rule until 1949, and it was the Dutch who were responsible for the introduction of paper money to Indonesia around 1900. Most of their issues prior to 1930 are scarce; later ones are much more common.

Japan occupied the islands from 1942 to 1945. Most of their occupation issues—inscribed in Dutch, Japanese, and later Indonesian—are fairly inexpensive, as is the currency of the Republic of Indonesia, formed in the late 1940s.

Much recent Indonesia paper money is of a high artistic order, with multicolored vignettes and designs inspired by native carvings. Sukarno, first president of the republic, was prominently featured on its currency until his overthrow in 1967. Indonesian bills show the effects of inflation during the Sukarno dictatorship, one of the reasons he was removed from office.

Canada

In many ways, Canadian paper-money issues parallel those of its neighbor, the United States of America. As in the United States, the first Canadian paper currency was an early development. Canada also saw a fair amount of private banknotes, then a unified currency system after the achievement of dominion status in 1867. Canada has even had several issues of fractional currency, and, of course, the country has long been on the dollar system, as has the United States.

There have been points of difference between the two countries, however. Canada has employed denominations that have never been used in American currency (a four-dollar note of 1892 and a twenty-five-dollar bill of 1935 are prime examples). Canadian currency has been more colorful and less conservative in design changes than United States issues. This is in direct contrast to Canada's coinage, which is even more static than that of its neighbor.

In a technical sense, Canadian paper money goes back even farther than that of the United States. In 1685, French authorities produced a series of handwritten notes on playing cards. These bills were issued to soldiers, and they were simply promises made by the governor to pay them the amount on each bill in coin, once a shipload of coinage arrived from France. The troops accepted them readily enough, and what started out as an emergency measure was retained for many years. This playing-card money is excessively rare, and virtually none of it is in private hands.

Nineteenth-century issues are much more obtainable. Prior to the unification of Canada, two types of currency enjoyed wide circulation. The first was scrip, or *bons,* promises to pay issued by merchants, railroads, or in the case of the note illustrated, a distillery. Most bons date from the late 1830s, when as a backwash of depression in the United States, orthodox coinage and tokens disappeared from circulation in Canada. This 1837 bon is interesting in that it was good for fifty cents, or one écu, or two shillings sixpence. Multiple denominations were necessary because Canada was not as yet producing its own money and was dependent on American and **114** British coins.

DISTILLERIE DE St. DENIS.

60 SOUS.   XXXXXX.

HALF A DOLLAR

No. 656

St. Denis,
22 Juillet, 1837.

A demande,
que, Nous pro=
au porteur, en
ayant cours a Montreal, UN ECU, en
sommes de pas moins d'une piastre.

pour valeur re=
mettons payer
billets de Banques

Wid. NELSON & Cie.

UNITED STATES OF AMERICA
50 C.

ON DEMAND for value received, We promise to pay to bearer, in current Bank Notes
of Montreal, TWO SHILLINGS and SIX PENCE currency, in sums not less than five shillings.

Bon pour 2 6d.   Imprimerie de Louis Perrault, à Montreal.   Good for 2s. 6d.

Besides bons, private banknotes saw widespread usage. This parallels the American paper-money experience, for this was the era of the "broken banks" in the United States, which will be discussed later. The notes depicted are representative of the entire series, which was produced well into the 1860s. The vignette on the Bank of Clifton issue was adapted from an earlier token for use in Ontario. The four-dollar denomination on the Colonial Bank of Canada note may be explained by the fact that the British pound was worth four dollars at that time, and British pounds circulated in Canada.

In 1867, Canada became a unified nation. Three years later, a determined attempt was made to provide the country with a unified coinage to replace the motley collection of American, British, and Mexican coins, locally made tokens, and wampum then in circulation. Initial production of Canadian coins could not keep up with demand, however, and Canadian authorities turned to fractional currency as a solution. The twenty-five-cent note illustrated dates from 1870, and small bills in this denomination were circulated until the mid-1930s. By that time, Canada had become self-sufficient in minor coinage.

In the late nineteenth century, the government chartered a number of private, note-issuing banks, and a few continued to print money into the 1930s. Their privileges were gradually taken over by the government, which was now printing paper money of its own.

▲ Montreal, bon for 2 shillings 6 pence or 60 sous, 1837.

▲ Top: dollar, 1917; bottom: 25 cents, 1870.   ▼ Two dollars, 1974.

Large-sized Dominion of Canada notes were produced from 1870 to 1935. All inscriptions on these bills were in English, and members of the British royal family or Canadian governors graced the front of each note, with a Canadian landmark on the reverse.

In 1935, the Bank of Canada was formed to handle the printing of paper currency, and its issues were soon carrying inscriptions in French and English, in an attempt to please the *Québecois,* descendants of the original French settlers in Canada. Canadian bills have been bilingual since that time—as have postage stamps, official documents, etc. Modern Canadian banknotes usually depict the reigning monarch or some other popular figure on the front and scenery on the back. Bills of each denomination are multicolored, with one color predominating.

116

The United States of America

The United States affords the hobbyist an overwhelming amount of collecting possibilities. Thus, it is best to divide United States issues into four categories, which roughly follow each other in chronological sequence: first American paper money (1690–1800); private, or broken-bank notes (1800–65); Civil War currency (1861–65); and modern United States issues (1865–present).

First American Paper Money. As previously discussed, Americans began experimenting with paper money in 1690. Economic necessity dictated their involvement with this new medium of exchange, but there were other considerations, too. Foremost among them was military necessity.

In peacetime, each colonial government took in enough revenue in kind and (if they were very lucky) in coinage to pay the bills, to perform the rather modest demands made on colonial governments. These arrangements were thrown out of balance in time of war, however, for Massachusetts and the other colonies were expected to train, equip, and put colonial armies in the field against the enemies of the Crown—usually the French, who owned Canada. The first in a long series of wars broke out in 1689, and the last of them ended in 1763. During the intervening period, Britain and France—and their colonials—fought each other about fifty percent of the time.

All of this warfare cost colonial governments a good deal of money, which under ordinary circumstances would have been impossible to raise. But a way around this was developed by Massachusetts and tacitly agreed to by the English. The colony would print paper money, which it promised to redeem at the end of the war. And once the war had ended, Britain would send over coinage to pay for expenses. This money would be used to retire the notes, or better yet, the notes could remain in circulation, since everyone knew that they could be redeemed if necessary.

So, each of the colonies printed paper to pay for wars, then left it in circulation to increase the money supply. As we noted earlier, paper faced the twin dangers of counterfeiting and inflation, but a monetary system based on paper currency, even with its attendant risks, was obviously far better than no **117** monetary system at all, which was the likely result if paper were removed from circulation.

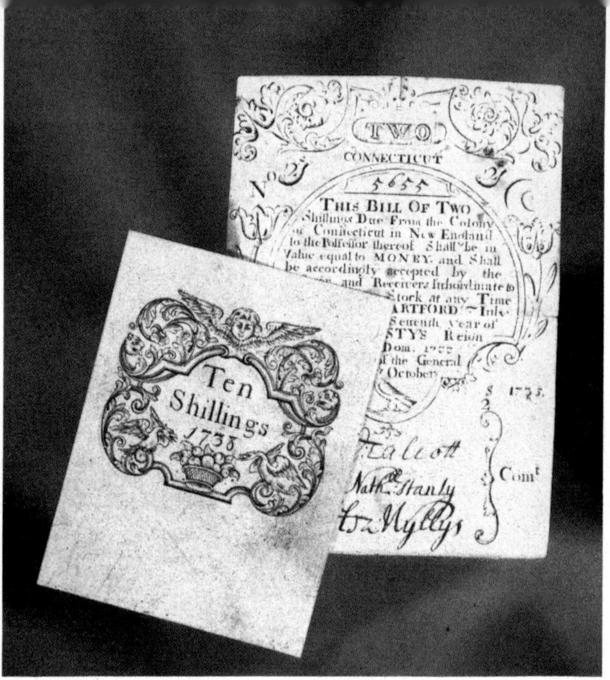

The format of American colonial paper money changed through time. The early, large-sized notes were generally printed from engraved copper plates. The 1735 two-shilling note from Connecticut is typical of these early issues. Since copper plate was exceedingly difficult to make in those days, old plates were often redated and reused when a new currency issue was authorized. The original date of the note illustrated is 1733, seen at the center; the new date of issue, 1735, can be seen to the right. Reverses tended to be rather simply done; this 1738 ten-shilling Rhode Island bill is representative.

By that time, many colonial issues were being printed from movable type, like books. Such a process was far easier than the old copper-plate method, and it was also somewhat more of a deterrent to counterfeiting. Typeset bills would be the rule in the remaining years of America's colonial status, and they would be used to fight the war for national independence as well.

New Jersey, 12 shillings, 1756. ▶

The 1756 New Jersey note is a typical product of the later colonial period. It employed fancy borders and odd bits of type to avoid falsification. The new, typeset bills were also smaller than the first colonial issues.

The coming of the American Revolution subjected American paper currency to immense strains. As usual, the costs of making war were to be covered by printing paper. This time, however, the British would not be there to redeem the currency at the end of the war. Moreover, the war lasted for eight years, far longer than any previous conflict.

Under these conditions, American currency began a downward slide. The 1779 eighty-dollar Continental (Federal) Currency note illustrates the problem. No denomination that large had ever been printed before, but by now the dollar had sunk in value to the extent that such a high-denomination note made sense. By 1780, Continental Currency was worth one-fortieth of its face value, and Congress gave up printing it.

Conditions were even worse in the individual states. They, too, printed paper money, and public faith in state currency declined even more rapidly than confidence in national issues. By 1781, it took one thousand dollars in Virginia paper money to purchase one dollar in coinage, and the situation in several other states was almost as bad.

Fortunately for the Americans, the shooting phase of the war ended in 1781, and after protracted negotiations a peace treaty

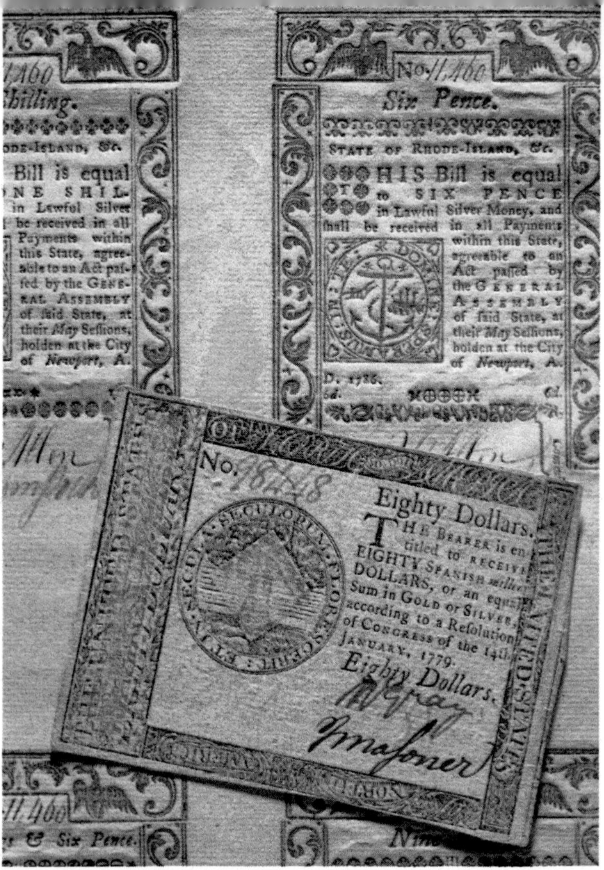

Shilling.

RHODE-ISLAND, &c.

Bill is equal
ONE SHIL-
in Lawful Silver
be received in all
Payments within
this State, agree-
able to an Act pas-
sed by the GENE-
RAL ASSEMBLY
of said State, at
their May Sessions,
holden at the City
of Newport, A.

No. 11,460

Six Pence.
STATE OF RHODE-ISLAND, &c.

HIS Bill is equal
TO SIX PENCE
in Lawful Silver Money, and
shall be received in all Payments
within this State,
agreeable to an
Act passed by
the GENERAL
ASSEMBLY
of said State, at
their May Sessions,
holden at the City
of Newport, A.

D. 1786.

No. 16848

Eighty Dollars.
THE BEARER is en-
titled to RECEIVE
EIGHTY Spanish milled
DOLLARS, or an equal
Sum in GOLD or SILVER,
according to a Resolution
of CONGRESS of the 14th
JANUARY, 1779.

Eighty Dollars.

& Six Pence.

Specie. K.   Specie. F.   Specie. B.

One PENNY   One PENNY   One PENNY

TWO   TWO   TWO

The PRESIDENT, DIRECTORS and Co. of the
BOSTON BANK   promise to pay
or bearer on demand   TWO DOLLARS
BOSTON
MASS

was signed in 1783. The American financial system was given time to revive. As it did so, it soon became apparent that paper money would play a different role in the independent United States than it had in the colonies. There were a few issues of state paper money in the early and middle 1780s, but these—and any ideas for a national paper currency—came to an abrupt halt with the Constitution of 1787. That document strictly forbade the states to print paper money, and it did not specifically say that the federal government could print it, either. The framers of the Constitution had no intention of risking another round of disastrous inflation, and most Americans agreed with them. It would take almost a century for the next federal and state currency to appear, and appropriately enough, it would take the biggest national crisis since the Revolution to produce it—the American Civil War.

What kinds of early American paper money are available to the collector? The first issues are all rare, and most known examples are in museums and historical societies. Some material from the late colonial period is available from time to time, but most of it is expensive. **121**

▼ Bank of the Republic,
5 dollars
(detail), 1852.

When we reach the period of the Revolution, there's a good deal more from which to choose. Continental Currency was printed in immense quantities, and a considerable amount of it has survived. State issues during the Revolution are also available at times, as are their counterparts, from the 1780s. None of this material is really inexpensive, although with perseverance and a bit of luck, it can be obtained for a modest outlay.

Private Banknotes. These issues occupy roughly the first two-thirds of the nineteenth century. They are often known as "broken" bank notes, since the banks issuing them collapsed during one of the periodic economic depressions. This was not always the case; descendants of some of these banks are still doing business today, but they no longer print paper money.

An essential characteristic of paper money in early nineteenth-century America is that it was *privately* produced. As we have seen, the Constitution did not allow state governments to print paper money, and it was unclear as to whether or not the federal government had that right. This early period was a time of tremendous growth, when the amount of capital needed to tame the frontier, build factories, dig canals, and construct railroads was far in excess of the amount of coinage available from the fledgling national mint or from abroad. If American expansion were to realize its full potential, some way of increasing the money supply would have to be found. Shortly before 1800, it was.

Bank of Commerce, 20 dollars (detail), 1861. ▶

Why not allow the individual states to charter *private* banks, and give them the right to issue notes against their cash reserves? The scheme looked feasible, and the first private, note-printing banks appeared just before the turn of the nineteenth century. Within fifty years there would be hundreds of them, representing virtually every city and town in the Union. The era of the broken banks had come to America.

The earliest private issues were fairly primitive. Like colonial paper money, many were printed from movable type. The 1789 sheet of four small notes illustrated from the Bank of North America is typical. Note the low denominations: at the time these bills were printed, there was a shortage of small change in the new nation. Incidentally, the paper for this issue was provided by none other than Benjamin Franklin.

Notes of this type were easy to counterfeit. By about 1805, someone came up with an elaborate, engine-turned design which, while homely, was more difficult to falsify. The Boston Bank two-dollar bill of 1825 shown here is a fine example of this type of early private paper. This bill was printed from an engraved plate, not type, a practice that would become the rule.

By the time the Boston Bank printed its two-dollar bill, more elaborate designs, employing small vignettes and fancy script, were coming into favor. The Bank of Augusta ten-dollar bill

still employed a simple, somewhat crude design, but the engraver was obviously trying to produce a more attractive note than its predecessors.

By the late 1830s, great changes had taken place: the three-dollar bill from a hotel in Illinois (in those days, firms other than banks also printed paper money) is very attractive, employing vignettes from mythology at center-top. This would be a recurring practice for years to come. The design also incorporated contemporary symbols: a covered wagon and one of the new-fangled steamboats. Notes were still printed in only one color, usually black.

Color came to American currency by 1850. Its use in the beginning seems to have been an afterthought: the red and green additions to the Bank of New York note have nothing to do with the overall design. But within a few years, color had

How early Americans made a living. Top to bottom: Tide Water Canal, 2 dollars, 1840; Bank of Chippeway, 5 dollars, 1838; Bank of Clifton, 5 dollars, 1838. ▶

▲ *Franklin Silk Company, dollar (detail), c. 1838.*

become an integral part of the printing process, and the years between 1850 and 1860 saw the production of some of the most beautiful paper money ever printed in America.

The money a group of people produce and use can tell us a tremendous amount about their livelihoods, their aspirations, their day-to-day lives. Paper money from the era of the broken banks is one of the best ways we have to look into the American past and see an entire people depicted, immobile, in a more than photographic reality.

The deep-seated sense of hard-won nationhood is present **125**

▲ *Farmers & Exchange Bank, 5 dollars (detail), 1861.*

on these notes, with representations of splendid, militant bald eagles and portraits of great American patriots. The working lives of Americans a century and a quarter ago find expression on these bills: illustrated here, we see Americans transporting goods and people on a raft, busy at work on the Baltimore waterfront, building a ship, farming the land. The main engraving on a one-dollar note of the Franklin Silk Company is prophetic, showing how Americans survived in older times—by farming—and a more modern way of making a living—as factory workers.

But a less happy, more disturbing side of life in America can be seen on these notes. The central vignette on a five-dollar bill from Charleston, South Carolina, shows a group of slaves that appear contented enough, picking cotton and transporting goods by wagon. But meantime a growing number of Americans were agitating for an end to the South's "peculiar institution," human slavery. Ten days after this bill was issued, the Civil War began. It began in Charleston, South Carolina, a mile or two from the Farmers and Exchange Bank. A way of life would pass away, and with it, the age of broken banks. This paper money remains, an eloquent witness of an earlier age.

Fortunately for the collector, the issues of the private, nineteenth-century banks are still available in large numbers, and it is possible to acquire a note in virtually unused condition for just a small investment. This is due in part to the fact that a good many of these banks were fiscally unsound, issuing more paper than they could possibly redeem. They were thus **126** ripe targets for collapse whenever an economic depression

▲ *Legal Tender Note, 2 dollars, 1862.*

occurred, and depressions *did* take place in nineteenth-century America—in 1819, 1837, 1857, and 1873. With each economic dislocation, hundreds of banks went under. Their bills were never redeemed and destroyed, which is why there are so many of them around to this day. No other branch of paper-money collecting offers so much, in terms of age, historical interest, and beauty, for so modest a price.

Civil War Currency. The American Civil War was the worst conflict the nation ever endured. It went deeper than previous and subsequent wars, which merely changed the relationships between nations. The Civil War altered the relationships between individual human beings, black and white, Northerner and Southerner.

It is only logical that a conflict which cut so deeply would bring other changes as well. In a sense, the war heralded the economic coming of age for the Northern states, pointing out the future paths of America's economic development. The ultimate reason why the North won and the South lost may be traced, not to superior generals or armies, but to the simple fact that the North had a well-developed industrial base that could be expanded astronomically to wage war, while the South did not. The war underlined the transition that was gradually taking place of the United States from a rural, agricultural society to an urban, industrial one.

The Civil War did not directly cause the end of the broken banks, but it definitely hastened it. A good many of these banks were in the South, of course, and when the Confederacy fell in the spring of 1865, the private banking system there collapsed **127**

▲ *National Bank Note, 2 dollars, 1865.*

along with everything else. Furthermore, the war brought tremendous prosperity to the North. But feverish speculation arising from that prosperity brought a major economic depression in the early 1870s, and most of the remaining private banks went under. At any rate, by that time there was a new kind of currency, a product of the federal government. The American people preferred it over private banknotes.

The new, national paper money was a direct result of the Civil War, and its introduction in 1861 stemmed from an unavoidable fact: if the federal government were going to wage a major war, it was going to need a good deal of money to do so. By 1864, it was costing the nation three million dollars a day to put down the Southern Confederacy, and, even back in 1861, costs were substantial, far more than anyone had believed possible. It was obviously going to be necessary to increase the money supply, whether the Constitution permitted it or not.

Congress got around the problem by passing an act that permitted the Treasury Department to circulate paper currency. Then, to make sure the paper circulated, it suspended specie payments. In other words, the new currency could not be redeemed in silver or gold. It had to be accepted in the

128

*Confederate States of America. Top:
5 dollars, 1861; bottom: 500 dollars, 1864.* ▶

belief that the money would one day be good. There was a good deal of grumbling by the public, but the new currency was accepted, and America's financial system had taken an essential step forward into the modern age. As in colonial times, the demands of war had produced an official paper-money system. And just as before, the new money worked well enough in time of war so that it was retained after the end of the conflict: all modern United States paper money can be traced back to the emergency issues of 1861.

The first national paper bills are called Demand Notes. This issue was relatively small, and it was followed in 1862 by a much larger printing of Legal Tender Notes (so-called from the inscription on the reverse) and by National Bank Notes in 1863. National Bank Notes were printed by the government, but issued by individual private banks all over the North, and eventually throughout the entire country. The federal govern-

ment granted chapters to certain banks, who were then allowed to print paper money against the par value of United States government bonds, which they were required to deposit with the government as security. This somewhat involved fiscal system remained in use until the Great Depression of the 1930s which saw the collapse of private American banks. Incidentally, a fair number of broken banks joined this system in the 1860s, which is one explanation for why they stopped issuing their own distinctive paper money. Legal Tender Notes are still produced, although only in one denomination, one hundred dollars.

Virtually all federal paper money of the Civil War period is extremely rare today, and when it is found, it is usually not in good condition. The only exception is Fractional Currency, small-sized notes of fifty cents or under. Their production commenced in 1862, and they were printed through the remainder of the war and well beyond the late 1870s. They were intended as a substitute for coinage, which people were hoarding due to their uncertainty about who would win the war. Fractional Currency can be quite attractive, and since many citizens kept the notes as souvenirs or curiosities, they are still available to the collector in fair numbers. Today they remain legal tender in the United States, as is all federal currency produced since 1861.

In addition to the new national currency, private banks continued to produce their own distinctive notes, although in smaller quantities than before. In addition, there was a large output of small-change bills (scrip) by private merchants, town authorities, and others. Many issues of scrip employed patriotic vignettes, for the war had created an upsurge of national fervor in the North.

The South entered the war with many disadvantages. The Confederate States of America (the name adopted by the breakaway, slave-holding states) did not contain any significant deposits of gold or silver. Even if they had, the sole modern mint in the area was in New Orleans, and that city fell to federal troops early in the war. All the same, the Confederate government had to put armies in the field, purchase supplies, **130** and pay its own expenses, and Southerners obviously had to

have some sort of money for daily transactions. So paper money was resorted to early on, and it would form the financial mainstay of war effort in the South for the next four years.

Early Confederate currency is fairly crude in appearance, and it is relatively expensive today. Until 1862, the war seemed to be staying within reasonable bounds, and the South was optimistic about a quick victory, followed by a return to peacetime conditions. So currency was printed in small amounts, and its value tended to remain high.

By the fall of 1862, however, it was apparent that the Confederacy was in for a long struggle if it was to make good its declaration of independence. By this time, moreover, it was by no means certain that it would succeed. Two things happened: the Confederacy expanded its paper-money production to pay the mounting costs of war, and inflation set in. As the money supply expanded beyond the South's capacity to absorb it, Sourtherners became increasingly skeptical about the Confederacy's ability to win the war and be in a position to redeem its currency. It is the issues of 1863 and 1864 that are most commonly encountered by collectors. As an indication of **131**

▲ Top: Mississippi. One hundred dollars,
  1862; 50 dollars, 1862.

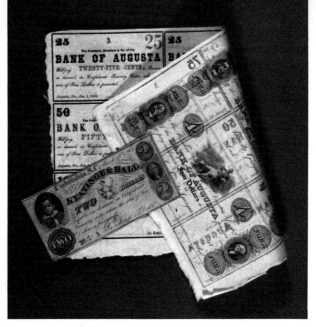

inflation, the South now had a five-hundred-dollar bill, beautifully printed but not worth very much. In 1864 alone, it has been estimated that the Confederate States of America printed two billion dollars worth of money.

And it was not only the Confederate government that printed paper money. So did the states, private merchants, and the old private banks. Under the Confederate Constitution, each state had the right to print paper money, and all of them did. There is probably almost as much of this state currency in existence as there is Confederate-printed paper. Two of Mississippi's issues are illustrated. The hundred-dollar bill was printed by the American Bank Note Company before the war had begun, which accounts for the quality. The fifty-dollar bill was printed in Mississippi itself; its primitive appearance is an indicator of the generally backward technology of the South at that time, a major factor in its defeat.

Private merchants and banks printed their own currency, just as they did in the North. The note illustrated is interesting because the firm that produced it, Keatinge & Ball, was also

132 responsible for most of the paper money issued by the Confed-

Top: National Bank Note, 20 dollars, 1923; bottom: Silver Certificate, dollar, 1923. ▶

◀ *Left: Keatinge & Ball, 2 dollars, 1864;*
right: sheet of Bank of Augusta 4-dollar notes,
c. 1840, used to print new notes in 1863.

eracy. And the crude, small-change notes of the Bank of Augusta were simply printed on the reverse side of an unissued sheet of banknotes printed twenty-five years earlier—the South was short of paper (along with everything else) and would use whatever came its way.

Most Confederate and Southern material is still readily available to the hobbyist, and these items, taken with their northern counterparts, form a very wide field of collectible American paper money.

Modern United States Issues. Since the end of the Civil War, the United States has issued several types of paper money, only a few of which are still collectible: National Bank Notes, Silver Certificates, Legal Tender Notes, and Federal Reserve Notes. At present, all United States paper, with the exception of the hundred-dollar bill, is in the form of Federal Reserve Notes. The hundred-dollar denomination appears as a Legal Tender Note and as a Federal Reserve Note.

National Bank Notes have already been briefly described. They are very popular with collectors today, due in part to their

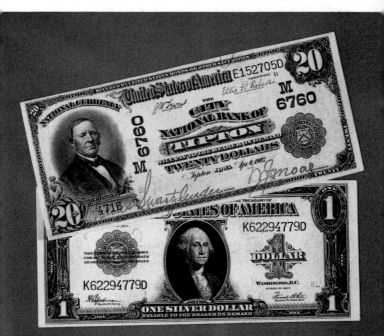

identification with cities and towns all over America. The 1903 twenty-dollar bill from Tipton, Iowa, is a particularly fine specimen of a National Bank Note. These bills were originally larger than current United States paper; like all other types of American currency, they were reduced in size in the late 1920s as an economy measure. The last National Bank Notes were those of the 1929 series.

Silver Certificates lasted into recent times. Originally introduced in 1878, they were printed in denominations ranging from one to one thousand dollars over the years, until their production was finally halted in 1968. Most collectible issues can be identified by the blue treasury seal and serial number, as illustrated on the 1923 dollar. Silver Certificates are occasionally still seen in circulation.

With the exception of the hundred-dollar bill, Legal Tender

Modern U.S. issues. Top: 1-dollar Federal Reserve Note (detail), 1963; bottom: central engraving on 1976 2-dollar bill, prepared for U.S. Bicentennial. ▼

Notes have departed from commerce. Notes of this type were first introduced during the Civil War, and they formed a backbone of the national financial system for the next century. Many earlier Legal Tender Notes were very attractive, employing patriotic vignettes, pictures of national heroes, and a black front/green back format which has been the rule on most United States currency.

Originally created to bring a semblance of order to a chaotic state of affairs in American banking, the Federal Reserve System has become virtually the sole producer of United States paper money at the present time. There are twelve Federal Reserve branch banks scattered around the country, and each issues paper money stringently backed by large reserves. At present, denominations printed range from one dollar to one hundred dollars, and they all closely resemble one another, except for the denomination. American patriots are depicted on the face, a design or a national monument on the back.

A current exception is the two-dollar bill. Issued in conjunction with the Bicentennial of American independence, the reverse of this bill depicts the signing of the Declaration of Independence. This is an indication that paper money is beginning to be used in a commemorative sense, a function coins have long enjoyed.

◀ *Unusual U.S. currency. Top: Gold Certificate, 10,000 dollars, 1908; bottom: National Gold Bank Note, 5 dollars, 1870.*

Latin America

Latin America produced its first paper money early in the nineteenth century. In the ensuing one hundred fifty years, this region has been responsible for some of the most interesting, strikingly attractive currency the world has seen. From the collector's viewpoint, Latin America is a rich field, for there are a great many old and modern bills available at nominal cost.

The largest element of this collecting area is Mexican paper money. In Mexico, the first currency issues came as a result of independence from Spain, a status achieved in 1821. The independent nation began as an empire, ruled by Agustin de Iturbide, the leader who had ejected the last Spanish garrisons. Styling himself Augustin I, he had himself proclaimed emperor in 1822 and had Mexico's first paper money printed to pay for his rather expensive tastes. The Mexican people soon tired of his extravagances, and he was overthrown in less than a year. Mexico became a republic, and the country's first experiment with paper currency came to an end. It would be many years before it would be repeated.

When paper currency was resumed in Mexico, it would take the form of private banknotes. The reintroduction of this form of money took place in the 1870s, and it was an indication that, after half a century of civil wars, foreign invasions, and a second empire, the nation had settled down to a relatively tranquil existence. It was now under the grip of Porfirio Díaz, who would be dictator until 1911. The Díaz government was exploitative and detested by a fair percentage of Mexicans, but it did bring a good deal of prosperity in its wake. This prosperity brought about a host of private, note-printing banks. Virtually all of their issues were printed in the United States or Britain. One of them, a thousand-peso bill from Yucatán is illustrated.

Díaz ruled Mexico for thirty-five years until he was overthrown in 1911. The next ten years saw the worst civil war in Mexico's history, as various elements jockeyed for position in the power vacuum remaining after Díaz' fall. This period is known as the Mexican Revolution, and it had a tremendous effect on the country's paper money.

All of the warring factions needed money, and all of them

▲ Mexico, two pesos, 1823.

had difficulty in obtaining it in orthodox ways. As a result, revolutionary groups throughout Mexico began printing paper money to finance their operations. This went on for several years, reaching a high-point in 1914–15.

The notes illustrated are typical. Many of them were primitive affairs, such as those issued by the Caballero Brigade. Bills of this type were printed like books, from movable type. The Constitutionalist Army five-peso note from Guadalajara is a more sophisticated example of military paper, but it is still rather crude compared to earlier, orthodox paper money. The leader of the Constitutionalist forces was Venustiano Carranza, and he would eventually become Mexico's legal president.

▲ Mexico (Yucatán). Banco Mercantil, 1,000 pesos, c. 1890 (specimen).

By now, the old private banknote system was in ruins, and many states took it upon themselves to supply their inhabitants with currency. The most widespread issues were those of Chihuahua, power-base of the bandit-soldier Francisco Villa. Villa, who was Carranza's most important foe through most of the period, printed enormous quantities of paper money of the type illustrated—so much, in fact, that even today you can purchase one in new condition for a small sum.

Carranza printed large amounts of his own currency, both in Mexico City and in Veracruz, where he had taken refuge from Villa's forces late in 1914. This period also saw the production of *cartones*, small cardboard notes that circulated as minor coinage in a period when people were hoarding the coins themselves.

The year 1915 was the turning point of the Mexican Revolution. Carranza's forces decisively defeated Villa, and peace slowly returned to the war-torn country. Carranza now had

Carranza currency. Top: Provisional Government at Veracruz, peso, 1915; center: Yucatán, carton for 20 centavos; bottom: an "infalsificable," 5 pesos, 1915. ▶

time to attempt a reform of the highly inflated revolutionary currency system. He had new multicolored notes printed in New York City, and old Constitutionalist paper could be exchanged for the new bills at a huge discount. Mexicans called the new issues *infalsificables* (money impossible to counterfeit), due to their ornate printing in several colors. Public faith in Carranza's new currency was strong enough to allow the bills to circulate at close to par. Mexico's paper currency was on the road to recovery.

In 1925, the Banco de México was formed. A governmental corporation, it was given sole control over issuing Mexican paper, a position it has enjoyed ever since. Until fairly recently, Banco de México notes were all printed in the United States. Since 1969, however, Mexico has produced its own banknotes, many of which are of outstanding quality. They depict national heroes on the obverse, a Mexican scene or piece of artwork on the reverse. The hundred-peso note, for example, portrays Venustiano Carranza who had, as we have seen, a large role in the history of Mexican paper money.

The issues of Central America do not go back as far as those of Mexico. There are certain parallels, however. Most notably,

▲ *Mexico, one hundred pesos, 1974*

▼ *Cuba. Top: peso, 1949; bottom: 20 pesos, 1891.*

there was an early reliance on private banks, whose bills were printed abroad, and a general trend toward governmental assumption of paper-money emission in subsequent years.

Outstanding among early Guatemalan paper-money issues are the multicolor notes from Quetzaltenango, dating from the turn of the century. After these bills arrived in Guatemala, they were stamped with an image of the national bird, the quetzal—which of course is where the town got its name. This stamp was a kind of local guarantee that the currency was genuine.

Many parts of Central America saw strong American penetration early in this century. Nicaragua was actually occupied for several years, and American financial influence, at least, is indicated by a 1912 Nicaraguan issue that gave the name of the bank in English and Spanish.

Some of the most attractive Central American banknotes have come from one of the smaller republics, Costa Rica. A

◀ *Central America. Top to bottom:*
Guatemala, 20 pesos, 1914; Nicaragua,
Córdoba, 1912; Costa Rica, 5 colones, 1969.

1969 five-colon issue from the government-operated Banco Central de Costa Rica has a multicolored mural as its reverse type. If Costa Rica wanted to produce a bill that could not be counterfeited, she succeeded.

Latin America includes a number of Caribbean islands, many of which have produced paper money. Early issues from this locale have included some notes of real historical importance; later productions are often outstandingly beautiful.

Cuba has been the source of some of the most fascinating historical issues. Notes of the first Cuban Republic depicted in the Introduction are still occasionally encountered, and many of them were actually signed by Manuel de Cespedes, the leader of the revolt against Spain. The latter had reestablished control of Cuba by 1878, and his power would last for exactly twenty years, until Spain lost the island in a war with the United States. During these remaining decades of the Spanish occupation, many private banks and public authorities supplied the island with currency. Paper money of independent Cuba closely resembles contemporary United States issues, in part because Cuban currency was printed in America **142** until after the Castro revolution.

▲ Top to bottom: Haiti, 2 gourdes, 1851; Bahamas, dollar, 1965; Jamaica, 2 dollars, 1976 (specimen).

▲ Top to bottom: Venezuela, 5 bolívares, 1968;
Colombia, 10 pesos, 1895; Colombia, peso, 1973;
Papayán, Colombia, peso, 1900.

Among other issues of Caribbean Latin America, those of Haiti deserve mention. Haiti was the first Latin American nation to gain her freedom, and she has always depended upon paper currency as a form of money. Newer nations such as Jamaica and the Bahamas are important to the collector of paper money because of their beautiful, multicolored issues, notes that set standards by which future paper currency will be judged.

Simón Bolívar was responsible for the freeing of northern South America from Spanish control. Today, Venezuela claims him as her national hero, as does Colombia. As a result, Bolívar has regularly appeared on the paper money of both nations, from the late nineteenth century to the present. The Venezuelan note illustrated is also a commemorative issue, celebrating the four hundredth anniversary of the founding of Caracas.

Colombia has used paper money somewhat more extensively than Venezuela, and her banknotes have tended to employ more attractive, imaginative designs. The 1895 ten peso is a fine example of a late nineteenth-century note, and it would be difficult to find a more colorful issue than the 1973 peso. In addition, Colombia has been the scene of a fair amount of provisional paper money, most of it dating from the Thousand Days' War (1899–1902), which devastated the country.

Virtually all of the currency of the Andean Republics (Perú and Bolivia) has been produced abroad, mainly in Britain and the United States. The thousand soles from a private bank in Perú is a superb example of the engraver's art as it was practiced a century ago. The central vignette appeared on a broken-bank note printed about ten years earlier.

Modern Peruvian notes have tended to be monochromatic, with a multicolored *guilloche* (an intricate, engraved design) in the center. Modern Bolivian paper currency often follows the same general design format, with local scenes and engravings of peasants, workers, and other citizens of Bolivia prominently featured.

Chilean paper money has been distinguished by a wealth of beautiful issues in the nineteenth century; in this century, it has

reflected one of Latin America's major problems—inflation. Chile was one of the first countries in Latin America to print paper money: national issues were produced from 1822–29. For the next fifty years, however, note production was in the hands of private banks, and it was not until about 1900 that the government once again enjoyed sole rights over production of Chile's currency.

By then, the inflation which has bedeviled the republic ever since was beginning to have its effect on the national paper money. The peso, Chile's monetary unit, steadily sank in value, and bills of higher and higher denomination were added to the currency series: a thousand-peso note by 1912, a ten-thousand-peso bill by 1932, and a fifty-thousand-peso bill by 1948.

In 1960, a currency reform took place, and a new monetary unit, called an escudo, now equaled one thousand old pesos. The collector will run across many Chilean peso notes surcharged with new escudo values, for it was not until 1962 that a new, definitive series of escudo notes was introduced. These bills are printed in Chile, and they often depict patriots on the front and scenes from Chilean history on the back. Inflation is still a major problem in Chile.

Argentina began printing paper money in the 1820s, and its nineteenth-century issues closely reflected the unsettled state **145**

▲ Top: Perú, 1,000 soles, c. 1866
(specimen); bottom: Bolivia, peso, 1962.

of affairs there. A brief, unsuccessful attempt at providing Argentina with a strong, centralized government produced the 1824 peso note illustrated. By 1830, each Argentine province was essentially independent, and many of them issued their own paper money; the ten-peso issue from Buenos Aires is typical.

Unification came to Argentina late in the nineteenth century, as cattle and grain production were creating the bases of future national prosperity. The united republic took over the emission of Argentina's currency from the welter of private banks and provincial authorities by the mid-1890s, and it has held this monopoly since that time. Like Chile, Argentina now prints her own paper money; like Chile, also, Argentina's currency shows the effects of twentieth-century inflation.

The paper money of the other River Plate republics may be more briefly described. Uruguay's issues date from the mid-nineteenth century, and none are particularly common. Since 1911, the Uruguayan government has been responsible for the country's paper currency. Most of it has been printed in Britain or France, and it often portrays José Artigas, hero of Uruguayan

▲ *Chile. Top: peso, c. 1865 (specimen); bottom: ½ escudo, 1962.*

independence. Paraguayan paper money dates from about the same time as the first Uruguayan issues, and the paper money of this country reveals a deep sense of national pride. A Paraguayan soldier appears on several modern notes, national heroes on others. Older Paraguayan paper was printed in the United States; more recent bills have been produced in Britain.

Brasilian paper currency dates from 1810. Its introduction at that time was part of a general campaign for modernization of the Portuguese colony. Paper money soon became a financial mainstay of the colonial government and, after 1822, of the independent Empire of Brasil.

The empire issued paper money in large quantities throughout its seventy years of existence, for the country needed all the capital it could acquire to build railroads, establish industries, tame the Brasilian frontier, and perform the other tasks that Dom Pedro II (1831–89) wanted accomplished. Unfortunately, his government sometimes put entirely too much paper into circulation, which led to periodic bouts with inflation.

Pedro II was overthrown in 1889. A republic was pro- **147**

▲ *Clockwise from top: Argentina, peso, 1834;*
100 pesos, c. 1975; Paraguay, 10 guaranies, 1952;
Argentina, 10 pesos, 1869 (specimen).

claimed, and it, too, produced large amounts of paper money, first in denominations based on the reis, and after 1941, on the cruzeiro (a cruzeiro equaled one thousand reis). Inflation continued to be a problem, one reason being that when Brasilia, the new capital of Brasil, was constructed in the 1950s and early 1960s, unsupported paper money was issued to pay for it. This led to political and social unrest, and it was one reason for the overthrow of the government in 1964 and the establishment of the present authoritarian regime.

In 1966, the new regime created a new cruzeiro, worth one thousand of the old. The note illustrated was one of the first issues under the reform, the new value merely being overprinted on an older bill. The central figure is Pedro II, who has been prominently featured on many bills of the republic—which is odd, considering that he was the man the republicans overthrew in the first place. Brasilian banknotes from the twentieth century are quite inexpensive, and some of their nineteenth-century counterparts are also within reach of the **148** average collector.

▲ *Brasil. Top: 1,000 reis, c. 1855; bottom: 100 cruzeiros, devalued in 1966 to 10 centavos.*

Building and Caring for Your Collection

Paper money can be collected in many different ways: some hobbyists may specialize in the currency of a particular country, others may prefer to collect specific kinds (inflation currency, invasion money, and the like), and still others may want to concentrate in notes portraying national heroes, landscapes, etc. Most collectors begin in a generalized way, eventually finding out that they like one area better than others, and then specializing in that field. You will discover that there is enough paper money available so that you can collect in almost any field.

Building a paper-money collection can be achieved in several ways. If you've decided to collect currency from World War II, for example, seek out another hobbyist with the same interest. Chances are he'll be only too happy to tell you about his paper money, perhaps even give you a few examples. If you're interested in the paper money of your own country, watch the money that you handle from day to day for anything odd, and ask local merchants to do the same. This is a highly effective way of adding to a collection.

If you travel abroad, save examples of the paper money you receive; ask your friends to do the same. Old books can be a source of finding paper money (people use bills for bookmarks), and so can antiques (an amazing amount of banknotes were shoved aside and forgotten in desk drawers when banks failed).

For modern issues, go to a foreign exchange company. This is an excellent, rather inexpensive way of obtaining crisp, new bills. Join a coin or paper-money club in your area. You will find such an organization a source of new material for your collection; more important, it's a way of sharing information and expanding knowledge of your hobby.

Finally, of course, you can always go to a coin dealer, most of whom have a sideline in paper money, and add to your collection that way. Buying from a dealer is by no means the cheapest method of building your collection, but it does have advantages, in terms of convenience and in time spent looking for a particular bill. In any event, prices for paper money are still fairly reasonable, even if you do buy them from a dealer. **149**

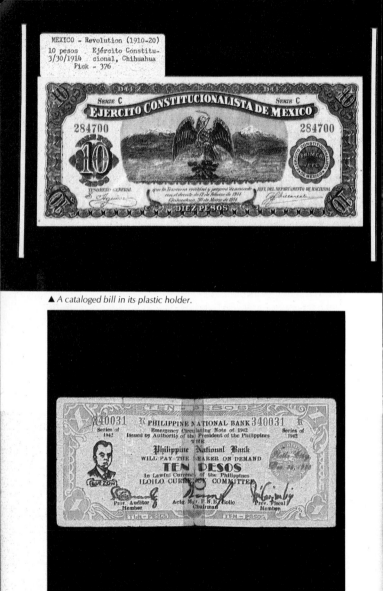

MEXICO – Revolution (1910–20)
10 pesos   Ejército Constitu-
3/30/1914   cional, Chihuahua
    Pick – 376

▲ A cataloged bill in its plastic holder.

▲ How not to repair paper money—the transparent
tape has discolored the bill.
A "reassembled" note in its plastic holder. ▶

But it is advisable to decide exactly what you want to collect *before* adopting that approach.

Until recently, the storage of paper money posed real problems for the collector. There were two basic ways of going about it, neither of which was satisfactory: mounting currency in an album, like photographs, with a photographic mount over each corner; or affixing them to album pages with stamp hinges. The first method only allowed you to see one side of the note, and if you tried to remove it, you risked tearing off a corner. The second method allowed you to see both sides, but the stamp hinges often left marks when they were removed. Neither method was very effective in keeping the notes from getting dirty, and the sulfur content of the paper album pages sometimes produced adverse chemical reactions with bills and printing inks.

These problems have been solved by the introduction of plastic, acetate, or polyvinyl chloride bill holders, made in a wide range of sizes, You can buy them by the page or for individual bills. Most coin dealers have them, as do many stamp dealers (hobbyists in that field use them for holding envelopes and postcards). The new bill holders will keep your notes flat, moisture- and dirt-free, and at least in the case of acetate ones, chemically inert. Thus, they will not affect a bill's paper or color.

Gummed labels are available from any stationery supply house. Affixed on the plastic holder, they can be used to give essential information about the note inside. The one illustrated is a typical example of how the system works.

Can you improve the appearance of your paper money? You can, although it's somewhat more difficult than it is with coins. But a bill can be washed in clear water, *providing* there are no signatures or serial numbers in ink. If there are, leave the bill as it is, for the handwritten parts will run. Once washed, the note can be placed between two pieces of blotting paper, and then dried. Stacking a few books on top will help remove any creases. Creases can also be minimized by ironing the bill, again between two places of blotting paper. In all cases, it's best to experiment with material of little or no value before attempting a more ambitious cleaning job.

◀ Collectible bills
vary widely
in condition, as
can be seen
by these Turkish 5-piastre
notes from 1917.

One of the inherent difficulties with paper currency is that it does not last forever. Large bills, particularly, tend to be folded and refolded for easier carrying. The folds develop into tears, and the bills may literally fall apart.

This poses a problem for the hobbyist: a bill in several pieces may not be the answer to a collector's prayers, but it is better than no bill at all. It may remain in a collection for years until a better specimen of the same issue can be found. Many collectors try to patch these bills back together, using transparent plastic tape. This type of repairing should be avoided: the tape may react adversely with the paper in the bill, and it can never be removed without causing even worse damage. The best way to handle the pieces is to position them in acetate holders, matching them up as closely as possible. Then look for another sample of the same bill—in one piece!

Appendix: Reading and Dating Paper Money

Collectors are often initially puzzled by paper money that bears inscriptions and dates in unfamiliar languages. This section, though it is not by any means comprehensive, will help to clear up some of the confusion. Most foreign paper money encountered will have denominations and dates based on one of the following numeric systems:

WESTERN	0	½	1	2	3	4	5	6	7	8	9	10
ARABIC-TURKISH	•	١/٢	١	٢	٣	٤	٥	٦	٧	٨	٩	١•
INDIAN	0	½	१	२	३	४	५	६	७	८	९	१०
BURMESE	၀	G	၁	၂	၃	၄	၅	၆	၇	၈	၉	၁၀
THAI-LAO	0	%	๑	๒	๓	๔	๕	๖	๗	๘	๙	๑๐
ORDINARY CHINESE JAPANESE-KOREAN	另	半	一	二	三	四	五	六	七	八	九	十
HEBREW			א	ב	ג	ד	ה	ו	ז	ח	ט	י

Denominations in these characters should pose no problems. Dates, however, can be troublesome. The year 1977 is 5737 in the Jewish calendar, so bills of the State of Israel should bear a date reasonably close to that figure, Israel's independent life having been a brief one. In the Buddhist era, 1977 translates to 2520, and a Buddhist dating system is used on some notes in the Indian subcontinent region. All this is based on a solar year.

However, a notable percentage of the world uses a lunar year, with an era beginning in 622 A.D. This is the practice of the Moslem world. Fortunately, it is fairly easy to calculate Western years from shorter Moslem ones. Since a lunar year is three percent shorter than a solar year, subtract three percent of the Mohammedan-era date (rounded to the nearest whole number) from that date and add 621. Thus, if you have a note

dated 1370 in Arabic, find three percent of 1370, rounded to

▲ Libya, 5 pounds, 1950. ▼ Greece, 1,000 drachmae, 1939.

the nearest whole number (41). Subtract this number from 1370 (1329), and add 621. The resulting number is 1950, the date of the note.

The rest of this section will give you an idea of the English equivalents for some of the non-Latin characters sometimes encountered on paper money.

China

Bank of China

行銀國中

Bank of Communications

行銀通交

Central Bank of China

行銀央中

Farmers Bank of China

行銀民農國中

Central Reserve Bank of China
(Japanese occupation)

行銀備儲央中

Federal Reserve Bank of China
(Japanese occupation)

行銀備準合聯國中

▲ *China, Bank of Communications, 10 yuan, 1914.*

People's Bank of China
(People's Republic)

Bank of Taiwan

臺 灣 銀 行

Greece

Bank of Greece
ΤΡΑΠΕΖΑ ΤΗΣ ΕΛΛΑΔΟΣ

Greek State Note
ΒΑΣΙΛΕΙΟΝ ΤΗΣ ΕΛΛΑΔΟΣ

National Bank of Greece
ΕΘΝΙΚΗ ΤΡΑΠΕΖΑ ΤΗΣ ΕΛΛΑΔΟΣ

Russia

State Credit Note
(Russian Empire and some
Civil War issues)
ГОСУДАРСТВЕННЫЙ КРЕДИТНЫЙ
БИЛЕТЪ

South Russia
(Civil War period)
ГЛАВНОЕ КОМАНДОВАНIЕ
ВООРУЖЕННЫМИ СИЛАМИ

Siberian Provisional Government
(Civil War period)
СИБИРСКОЕ ВРЕМЕННОЕ
ПРАВИТЕЛЬСТВО

КАЗНАЧЕЙСКIЙ ЗНАКЪ

Ukrainian People's Republic
(Civil War period)
УКРАИНСЬКА НАРОДНЯ РЕСПУБЛИКА

State Bank Note
(USSR)
БИЛЕТ ГОСУДАРСТВЕННОГО БАНКА
СССР

Index

Special Offer

If you enjoyed this book
and would like to have our catalog
of more than 1,400 other Bantam titles,
including other books in this series, just
send your name and address
and 25c (to help defray
postage and handling costs)
to: Catalog Department, Bantam Books, Inc.,
414 East Golf Rd., Des Plaines, Ill. 60016.

Dr. Richard G. Doty is Associate Curator of Modern Coins and Paper Money at the American Numismatic Society in New York City. A Fulbright scholar and former history teacher, Dr. Doty has published numerous reviews and articles and is associate editor of *Studies on Money in Early America*.